House Beautiful

750 Designer Secrets

HouseBeautiful

750 Designer Secrets

Exclusive Design Ideas from the Pros

from the Editors of

House Beautiful Magazine

Text by Kate Sloan

Hearst Books
a Division of Sterling Publishing Co., Inc.
New York

Library of Congress Cataloging-in-Publication Data is available.

Photography credits are listed on pages 442–445. The publisher has made every effort to properly credit the photographers whose work appears in this book. Please let us know if an error has been made, and we will make any necessary changes in subsequent printings.

10 9 8 7 6 5

Published by Hearst Books
A Division of Sterling Publishing Co., Inc.
387 Park Avenue South, New York, NY 10016

www.housebeautiful.com

Distributed in Canada by Sterling Publishing
c/o Canadian Manda Group, 165 Dufferin Street
Toronto, Ontario, Canada M6K 3H6

Distributed in the United Kingdom by GMC Distribution Services,
Castle Place, 166 High Street, Lewes, East Sussex, England BN7 1XU

Distributed in Australia by Capricorn Link (Australia) Pty. Ltd.
P.O. Box 704, Windsor, NSW 2756 Australia

Designed by Liz Trovato

Printed in China

Sterling ISBN 13: 978-1-58816-476-6
ISBN 10: 1-58816-476-4

For information about custom editions, special sales, premium and corporate purchases, please contact Sterling Special Sales Department at 800-805-5489 or specialsales@sterlingpub.com.

Introduction

As I travel around the country speaking to readers of *House Beautiful*, I am always impressed by the passion that so many people have when it comes to their homes. Often these feelings have little to do with specific furnishings, and everything to do with a sense of place, of security, of comfort. To be sure, this passion includes decorating. While many homeowners don't necessarily consider themselves decorators, they certainly know what they want for their homes and their families.

Even so, we all need help and advice from time to time. As the editor in chief of *House Beautiful,* I have the privilege of spending much of my time with designers, who are among the most creative people I have ever met. The best of them share a common trait: they put their clients' wishes first and foremost, while at the same time helping them achieve the look they want for their rooms.

Most designers have secrets of decorating based on years of experience and their own instincts. The goal of this wonderful new book is to share the best of these secrets in a format that is both beautiful and functional. After all, a great house isn't just about the look, it's also about how it works for the people who live in it. If you have children, for instance, you want ideas that allow you to have a home that is beautiful, yet "kid friendly" and comfortable. In essence, the only perfect house is the one that is right for you—not a house that is someone else's idea of how you should live.

To help you achieve your own goals at home, this book offers you 750 design secrets that together cover just about every decorating dilemma that faces us, and offers solutions in every case. You will find advice on pulling a room together, decorating in small and odd spaces, displaying your collectibles and art, and tips on everything from entertaining to lighting.

There are little details that always matter, such as secret 352: "No kitchen should be designed without under-cabinet lighting." Big ideas are here, too, like secret 25: "To help create balance and scale, use symmetry—pairs of pictures, sconces, chairs, etageres." This book is ideal for the millions of people who possess a passion for decorating but cannot afford a designer, or simply for those who choose to do their decorating themselves. In these pages, you will see the best work of some of the most talented designers from across America, and in the process, discover "how they did it."

I hope this book becomes the ultimate companion in your endeavors to decorate your home with passion.

Mark Mayfield
Editor in Chief, *House Beautiful*

Chapter One

Style and Lifestyle

1

"Low upholstered pieces in a room with high ceilings add grandeur."

—Mariette Himes Gomez

Designing a room involves balancing possibilities with reality, dreams with budgets, and style with lifestyle. Whether you're decorating a city apartment or a country weekend cottage, a new suburban home or an old townhouse, understanding your dwelling's architecture is as important to developing its decor as is coming to terms with your daily routines.

Experts may not always agree on the constituents of good design, but their collective insights can provide a useful road map to the process of fusing the tastes of two different people or the advantages of mixing furnishings from two different centuries. Once you learn how big a chair a certain room can tolerate, when to employ symmetry and when to break from it, how to arrange furnishings to create comfortable conversation zones, or how to balance the scale of a pair of side tables with a classically proportioned room, you're ready to craft a character-filled room of your own—or work with a pro to help you with one.

2

"In a palatially proportioned room, include enough upholstered pieces to keep voices from echoing."

—*Frank Babb Randolph*

Section One

The Big Picture

3

"A lot of well-known designers race toward a finish line, but finished to us means stale—we love rooms that are off or even a little wrong."

—John Dransfield and Geoffrey Ross

ROYAL STYLE

4

"Talking to the architect about where the electrical outlets will go and what kind of window casements would be best means you can troubleshoot a lot of potential problems at the beginning rather than trying to come up with solutions later."

—*Tim Clarke*

5

"If you've got a great view of nature, install surfaces and furnishings made of materials like steel, stone, wood, and glass, which defer to the colors and textures of the landscape."

—*Page Goolrick*

6

"The most important thing is what you feel when you walk into the room."

—*Benjamin Noriega-Ortiz*

7

Rules are made to be broken as long as you do so with style.

8

"Change nothing just for the sake of change."

—*Kelly Harmon*

9

"A vacation house should be relaxed and easy to live in."

—*Dan Carithers*

10

"A home should always be a portrait of its owners."

—Bobbie McAlpine

11

"Not interfering with views is Decorating 101."

—Scott Salvator

12

"Use a work of art as the starting point for a scheme."

—Scott Salvator

13

Enlist an architect and interior designer at the same time for the best results.

17

"You don't need a lot of elements to create a dynamic effect."

—Jeffrey Marks

18

"I like mixing features of high and low style."

—Tom Scheerer

19

"I don't believe in decorating a home all at once."

—Rita Konig

14

"Create a look that's refined—but still alive—by blending 250-year-old antiques with bursts of mid-century modern and pieces from Crate & Barrel."

—Tom Scheerer

15

"Allowing life to unfold in a house is more important than having the perfect pillow."

—Victoria Klein

16

"Don't shy away from the the Old-World notion of benign neglect."

—Victoria Klein

20

Let the eccentricities of a house provide a palette upon which to layer elements of your own personal vision.

21

"A sense of appropriateness is one of the hardest things to achieve."

—David Netto

22

"An apartment is like a second skin—if it feels like a good cashmere sweater when you are inside, then it's right."

—Jean-Louis Deniot

23

"I love the vein of great American decorating that isn't flashy, like the approach of Billy Baldwin and Parish Hadley."

—David Netto

24

"Establish atmosphere and identity with themes, such as Italian, Swedish, and Chinese rooms."

—William Holloway

Section Two

Understanding Scale and Proportion

25

"To help create balance and scale, use symmetry—pairs of pictures, sconces, chairs, etageres."

—Victoria Neal

PERIOD ROOMS
GREAT HOUSES OF ENGLAND & WALES
GREAT IRISH HOUSES
CASTLES

26

"In a large living room, mix antiques with bold color and modern fabrics to achieve balance."

—Anthony Baratta and William Diamond

27

Generous proportions and repetitive details create high drama.

28

Capture the allure of English country houses with a mixture of elegant comfort and slight disarray.

29

"Ideally the table before the sofa would be just a little lower than the seat of the sofa."

—Dorothy Draper

30

Anchor a large room with a sense of symmetry.

31

"You can't put dinky antiques in a large space."

—*Jeffrey Marks*

32

"Create balance with a mix of varied but compatible furnishings."

—Thomas O' Brien

33

"I edit rigorously for scale, form, and color."

—Celeste Cooper

34

"Try something different when the site dictates it."

—Barbara Barry

35

Strive for harmony and balance with pairs of things—chairs, vases, sconces—then throw in something offbeat to keep the ambience from getting stiff.

36

"Mix new pieces with old, modern with traditional, as a way to bridge the differing tastes of two people in one household."

—*Michael Misczynski*

37

"Edit your furnishings—sometimes you need to take something away rather than add."

—*Jeffrey Marks*

38

"When pieces are too evenly matched, you can lose the sense of how special each thing is."

—*Frank DelleDonne*

39

"Complement spacious interiors with large-scale furnishings, antiques, and art."

—*William Hodgins*

40

"Forgo perfect symmetry in an oval space."

—Paul Wiseman

41

A monochrome palette makes a room seem larger.

42

"Mix crafted and detailed furnishings, fabrics, and accents in unexpected ways."

—Victoria Klein

43

"Paired columns framing a centered fireplace in a living room demand a symmetrical seating arrangement."

—Kerry Joyce

44

"There's nothing worse than choosing everything at the same level of fanciness."

—Tom Scheerer

45

"Whether your style is formal or casual, your rooms have to function for you—some people like to slouch together on soft upholstery, others like to sit alone with more support."

—Paul Wiseman

46

"The scale has to agree: don't swamp a fragile antique side chair with a voluminous sofa."

—Mariette Himes Gomez

47

Choose overstuffed sofas and generous slipper chairs to make a smallish room look bigger.

48

"Take cues from your art and select furniture that complements it."

—Joe Nahem

LONDON
ROBERT DOISNEAU

49

"You don't always need twins to create a sense of balance."

—Mariette Himes Gomez

50

"In a room of modest proportions, take the furniture up in scale to create impact."

—Frank Faulkner

51

"Be sure accent pieces, such as sconces, pillows, and side tables, are commensurate in scale with upholstered pieces."

—Martyn Lawrence-Bullard

Section Three

All About Furniture

52

"Incorporate a common thread—such as a neutral color—to unify eclectic furnishings."

—Kelly Harmon

53

"When a room doesn't come with good architectural features, use a pair of boldly shaped chairs to lend it structure—they bracket a space and create a sense of place within the room."

—Mariette Himes Gomez

54

"Update a pair of period armchairs with unexpected mohair velvet upholstery in a sunny pistachio color."

—Jean-Louis Deniot

55

"Jazz up an old table base with a white acrylic top."

—Benjamin Noriega-Ortiz

56

"Wood—painted, gilded, or natural—adds gentle warmth."

—Jean-Louis Deniot

57

"Don't be overly concerned with using pedigreed pieces."

—*Benjamin Noriega-Ortiz*

58

"Let heirloom pieces star amid a palette of discreet colors, soft prints, clean-lined upholstery, simple floor coverings, and minimal window treatments."

—*Susan Ferrier*

59

"Arrange furniture according to patterns of foot traffic, with seating groups stationed throughout a room."

—*Victoria Neal*

60

"A smattering of antiques adds tremendous personality to a room."

—*Eric Cohler*

61

"Give Continental flair to a dining room by combining American Windsor chairs and an old barnwood table with an Italian chandelier and oversize mirror."

—Dan Carithers

62

"Build excitement by setting up a willful confrontation of styles."

—Joe Nahem

63

"Order big pieces first and leave the details until the end."

—Tim Clarke

64

When it comes to French antiques, it helps to know your Louis: If the lines are heavy and straight, the object is Louis XIV; slender, scrolled, and curved, Louis XV; straight and elegant, Louis XVI.

65

Several inviting seating areas make a large space more comfortable.

66

"Add a touch of luxury to a guest bath with a slipper chair and an Oriental rug."

—Mary McDonald

67

"Create tableaux of provocative shapes by making artistic juxtapositions of recycled furnishings and other pieces of ostensible junk."

—Adam Dolle

68

"The wonderful thing about Gustavian furniture is that it's at once elegant and relaxed."

—Edie van Breems

69

Improvise an affordable coffee table in a summer house by pushing two benches together.

70

Being eclectic means feeling comfortable about putting an antique bench with a Crate & Barrel armchair.

71

"Furniture seems to dance on a light floor."

—Frank Babb Randolph

72

"Have the confidence to complete your scheme to a point that leaves room for further collecting."

—Katie Ridder

73

"If you're on a tight budget, splurge on a superbly built sofa—everything else can come from Pottery Barn."

—Thomas Beeton

74

"An antique such as a Windsor chair, which is spare in itself, can work beautifully with a piece with contemporary lines."

—Dan Carithers

75

"Add a conservative touch to a contemporary room by introducing an antique or two—such as a pair of diminutive Regency corner chairs."

—Tom Scheerer

76

"A pied-a-terre is not the place for collections of great art, antiques, sculpture, or books, but should, rather, like a custom-designed hotel suite."

—John Oetgen

77

"Invite scrutiny of graphic pieces of furniture by including only a few of them in a room."

—David Kleinberg

78

Fill your rooms with furnishings and objects that have tales to tell.

79

"Unite cosmopolitan clusters of furniture with lots of luxurious materials and mysterious colors."

—John Oetgen

80

"Update a formal look with contemporary fabrics and some unexpectedly modern touches."

—Amelia Handegan

Chapter Two

Decorating with Color and Pattern

81

"Add additional zest to a bold-hued room with a potpourri of patterned pillows and a harlequin-pointed sofa skirt in a boldly striped fabric."

—Merrill Stenbeck

A room's palette should underscore its architecture, while its patterns should add visual intrigue. The combination of the two should make you feel at ease.

When choosing colors remember that context is key. Intense, saturated hues that stand up beautifully to tropical sunlight can look garish in northern environments or areas where the sky is overcast most of the time. Keep in mind, too, that regardless of where you live, different aspects of the colors in your rooms will be revealed as the natural light shifts over the course of the day and by lamplight.

At the same time, it's essential to honor your own taste in color. Add energy with jolts of spirited color in limited doses or establish serenity with a composition of pale, complex hues like chamomile, vanilla, and sage. Balancing the values (degree of lightness or darkness) and hues will allow you to bring various colors together harmoniously. Patterned fabrics, wallpaper, and carpets can serve as gracious links between different colors and give them spatial dimension.

82

"Brighten a dark, richly colored room with large mirrors."

—Benjamin Noriega-Ortiz

83

Not everyone can sleep in a red bedroom.

Section One

Defining Ambience and Creating Character with Color

84

To offset the intensity of a strong wall color, choose a light rug such as a natural flokati or a sea grass mat.

BAUHAUS
New York Interiors
NEW YORK 1960
HISTORY OF ART

85

Use a bold color sparingly to punctuate a room.

86

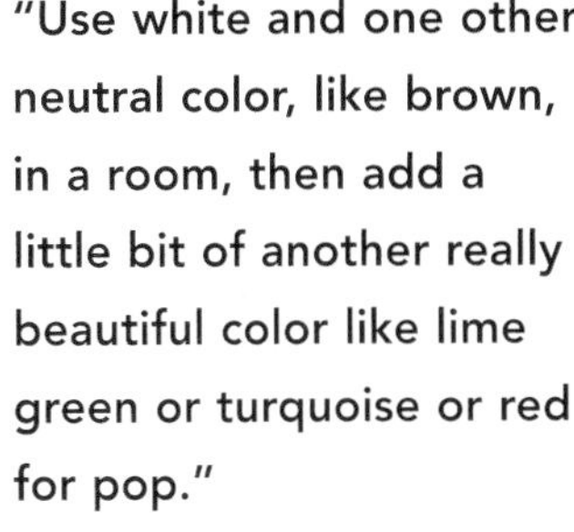

"Use white and one other neutral color, like brown, in a room, then add a little bit of another really beautiful color like lime green or turquoise or red for pop."

—*Doug Meyer*

87

For a soothing quality, use different values of the same hue.

88

In a small home, choosing a single color helps expand the sense of space and create a flow from room to room.

89

"Be bold in small doses."

—*Jeffrey Marks*

90

"If you look out at the waves in the ocean or the grains of sand on a beach, it's very calming because you're seeing infinite variations on the same theme."

—Barbara Barry

91

"Set off clean, sculptural furnishings with pumpkin-colored walls."

—Benjamin Noriega-Ortiz

THE AMERICAN CENTURY
Palm Beach Houses
ITALIAN SPLENDOR

92

"Stick with shades of one gorgeous hue, such as shell pink, cinnabar red, or powder blue, and set them off with flattering neutrals like chocolate brown accents and a creamy foundation."

—Randall A. Ridless

93

"For adjacent rooms, select shades one rung away from each other on the color ladder of a paint card."

—Scott Sanders

94

In a small room, keep the number of colors to a minimum, but make sure the main color is a strong one.

95

"I love rooms that are red and white—paint all the furniture white, throw red upholstery on something, and call it a day."

—Doug Meyer

96

"Create coherence by combining eclectic furnishings with strong color."

—Benjamin Noriega-Ortiz

97

"To maintain serenity, avoid high contrasts—establish a rich variation within a narrow tonal range."

—Mariette Himes Gomez

98

"In a basement or windowless room, use oranges and neutral browns that stand up to low light levels."

—Victoria Neal

99

"Take a chance with an intense color—if you don't like it, just repaint it."

—Benjamin Noriega-Ortiz

100

"Red—in variations from cranberry to coral—is the most personality-packed part of the color wheel and gives a room zing like no other hue."

—Elaine Griffin

101

To reproduce historic colors, take a fragment to a vendor who can scan it and then custom-mix a match.

102

"Use warm colors to keep large rooms from feeling intimidating."

—Neil Korpinen and Rick Erikson

103

"In a setting filled with bright, saturated sunlight, incorporate furnishings and accents with 'the orchid colors' of Hawaii."

—Neil Korpinen and Rick Erikson

104

"Instead of redesigning a kitchen, update it by painting the walls and floors a fresh color."

—Kim Freeman

105

"I like using colors that don't exactly go together; I aim for an undecorated look."

—Russell Bush

106

Take a risk in a powder room—paint it chartreuse.

107

"I like colors you can't name—everything you look at should have something subtle going on."

—John Oetgen

108

"Enliven a stuffy Spanish-style house with dazzling paint colors—pale lilac, saffron yellow, or dusty willow-green."

—Robin Bell

109

"Boldly stain new wooden chairs to match an antique Chinese lacquer screen."

—*Christina Girard*

110

For visual amplification, choose the dominant and accent colors for one room, then reverse them in an adjacent room.

111

Let a work of art serve as the starting point for a palette.

112

"In a summer house, use a classic color combination of white and blue in any shade, from indigo and navy to periwinkle and delphinium."

—*Bob Andrews*

113

Enliven a pale neutral palette with jolts of color.

114

"Color can never be too strong in Florida because of the light."

—William Diamond

115

"Create an all-white room only where steady sunlight will pour through windows and greenery is visible all around."

—Kerry Joyce

116

"Sunflower yellow is too strong for an ordinary room, but in a white over-scale space it gets toned down by all the air around it."

—T. Keller Donovan

117

"A color scheme of natural greens—from gray and sage to celadon and teal—is nuanced and changes from morning to night."

—John Saladino

118

"In a kitchen, incorporate colors like pumpkin, sage, and citron that are good enough to eat."

—Connie Beale

119

"I think color is energy, but if you have too much energy in a space it's enervating—hold the color punch to 25 percent, then use neutrals for the rest."

—*Mary Douglas Drysdale*

120

Paint the walls of an entry hall a watermelon hue to form a lush backdrop for an antique table.

Section Two

Pattern 101

121

Anchor a white-walled room with a striped Indian dhurrie rug.

122

Layer small-, medium-, and large-scale patterns together.

123

"Technology has made stripes and geometrics more exciting than before."

—Charles Faudree

124

"Flowers should be in vases, not on fabrics."

—Barclay Fryery

125

"Allow your decor to be informed by an array of inspirations—the intricate patterns of interiors depicted in French Impressionist paintings, the work of Bloomsbury artists, the unabashed extravagance of Venice and India, or the beautiful decay of autumn gardens."

—Victoria Klein

126

"I often use a large-scale print on small-scale upholstered furniture."

—Tom Scheerer

127

"All the straight lines of striped fabrics need a bit of contrast, so couple them with nailhead trims when using them as upholstery."

—Carl Dellatore

128

"Choose prints you can live with for a long time and not tire of."

—*Oscar de la Renta*

129

"Pattern for me is all about texture—a suede sofa against against grass-cloth, or birch logs stacked against the chevron brick of a firebox."

—*Eric Cohler*

130

"Use brightly colored ikats or floral linens to take the edge off a room and convey a sense of softness and comfort."

—*Celerie Kemble*

131

"Intriguing textures—stone, sisal, linen, silk—can divert the eye and offer a substitute for complicated pattern."

—*Jose Solis Betancourt*

LE CORBUSIER A PARIS
LE CORBUSIER A PARIS
THE BEATLES ANTHOLOGY

132

"Lavish pattern on walls, curtains, and throw pillows to fill up space in an enormous room."

—Gary McBournie

133

Create a focal point by using a large-scale pattern in a confined area such as an alcove.

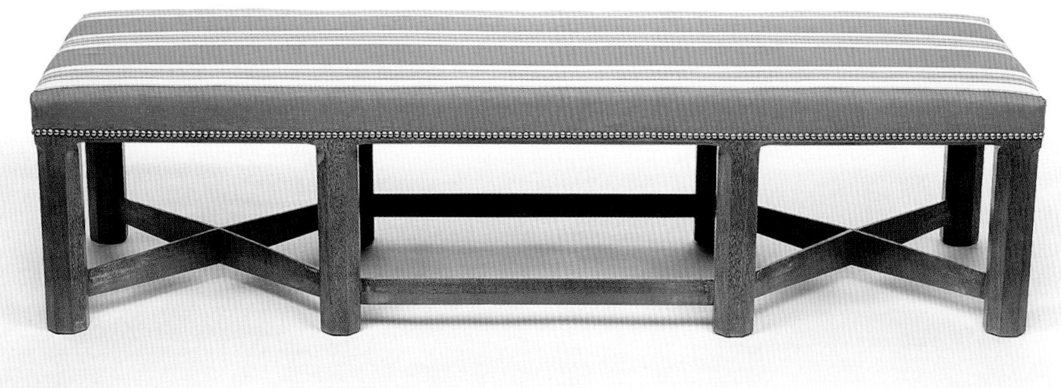

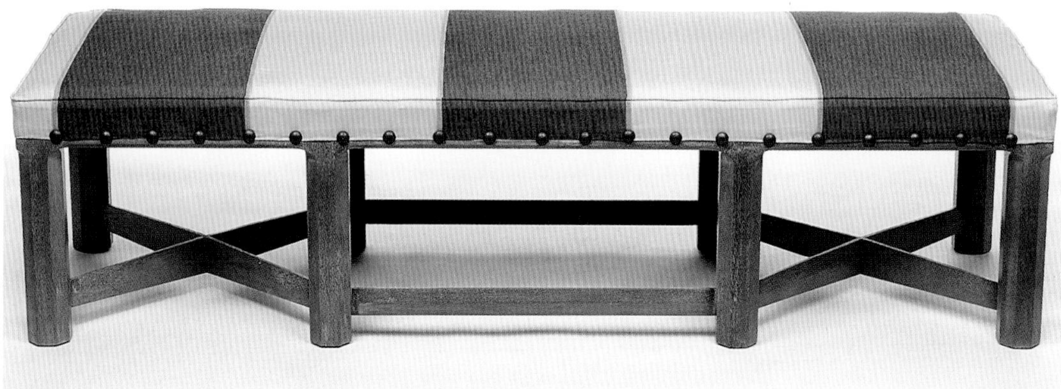

134

"When upholstering a long bench with a striped fabric, railroad—run the stripe along the length of the bench—if the stripe is of medium scale; place it across the frame if the stripe is very wide or very thin."

—*Carl Dellatore*

135

"Pattern has its place in carpets and wall coverings as opposed to fabrics."

—*Arthur Dunnam*

136

"Give a pool house exotic, hippie flavor by covering the windows, walls, and sofa with inexpensive hand-blocked Indian bedspread fabric."

—*Michael Smith*

Section Three

Mixing Color and Pattern

137

Bring a whimsical touch to a subdued, stately room with side chairs covered in hot-pink and apple-green Chinese silk brocade.

138

"Enliven a butler's pantry with checkerboard floors and apple-green walls."

—William Holloway

139

Add flavor to a guest room with toile de Jouy wallpaper and bed canopies made from a boldly striped fabric.

140

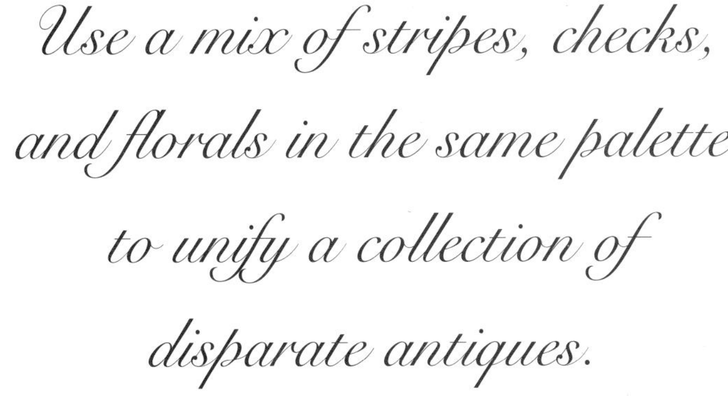
Use a mix of stripes, checks, and florals in the same palette to unify a collection of disparate antiques.

141

"Paint a cane chair the dominant color in a patterned carpet and cover a bevy of throw pillows in floral and striped fabrics that incorporate the same hue."

—Tim Clarke

142

"Use less pattern in more important ways and more color in less important ways."

—T. Keller Donovan

143

Enliven a room defined by a pale, restrained palette with just a couple of boldly patterned elements such as a floor painted with strong stripes and cushions with large embroidered leaves.

144

Choose a bold, blue-and-white striped rug to contrast with the small floral patterns of a china collection in the same hues.

145

Pale-colored fabrics with strong stripes and simple checks lend Scandinavian-inspired punch to a room painted in a serene hue.

146

Indulge a passion for color and pattern by covering the walls of a small dining room with red-and-white toile de Jouy, and topping the table with bright red linens.

147

Fabrics in zesty citrus shades of orange and lime with bold geometric patterns brighten neutral rattan furnishings.

148

To create a sense of progression, carry one color of a pattern into an adjoining room.

149

"Play with color and pattern to take a formal living room to a delightful extreme."

—Anthony Baratta and William Diamond

150

"Enliven a neutral room with lots of subtle patterns and a touch of red."

—Kathryn Ireland

151

"I use softer, deeper historical colors coupled with more texture and less pattern."

—Nancy Braithwaite

152

"A mix of graphic patterns in a monochromatic scheme conveys a sense of order and ease."

—*Thomas Pheasant*

153

Give an anteroom graphic appeal by setting upholstery in patterned fabric against spare walls painted a bold color.

Chapter Three

Shaping the Shell

154

"Add drama to a staircase with Honduran mahogany paneling and an elaborate fretwork stair rail."

—Kelly Wearstler

The decor of any room begins with its shell—the walls, ceiling, and floor. If you're fortunate enough to have a room with good bones, changing the atmosphere can be simple—just repaint the walls in a delicious color like vanilla, caramel, or chocolate or introduce drama with a rich damask or picturesque toile du Jouy wallpaper. If on the other hand, your room has damaged walls or ceilings or lacks spatial integrity, you may have to strip it down to its essence, move a wall or add architectural features to bring out the best in its character.

Either way, materials set the tone. Create a contemporary backdrop by applying a crisp skim coat of plaster or a sense of age by heavily troweling it. Introduce elegance with honed marble floors or rustic warmth with rugged ceiling beams.

Doors and windows speak volumes about a room's character, too. Hardware, like an antique brass knocker or a sleek stainless-steel handle, is as important to enhancing an atmospheric attitude as the size or material of the door itself. Ditto for the soft elements. Do you crave a sense of grandeur? Then dress the windows with puddling silk draperies. Are you a dyed-in-the-wool minimalist? Choose a crisp Roman shade or simple silk panels instead.

And don't forget the character-changing power of moldings—plaster crowns, baseboards, chair- and plate-rails—as well as architectural features like columns, pilasters, and wainscoting.

155

"Cover the windows of a summer house with simple, no-fuss Roman shades."

—*Lynn Morgan*

Section One

Walls, Columns, Millwork, and Molding

156

"In an old house with pedigree, recover as many authentic elements as possible while modernizing where necessary."

—Sam Blount

157

Create a seamless look by covering doors as well as walls with wallcovering.

158

"Create an ode to Jean Michel Frank by applying parchment squares to walls and glazing them in sepia."

—*Eric Cohler*

159

Search for a beautiful mantelpiece in architectural salvage yards.

160

"Add richness and depth to walls with Venetian stucco."

—*Scott Salvator*

161

"Accentuate a graceful stair hall with a faux stone treatment."

—Sam Blount

"Add interest to a large open space with natural materials and intriguing textures."

—Neil Korpinen and Rick Erikson

163

"Make furnishings and accents made of wood, velvet, shell, leather, and ceramic appear more sensual by applying monochromatic hand-troweled plaster and a coat of beeswax to the surrounding walls for a sense of aged smoothness."

—Michael Misczynski

HAMPTONS
STUDIOS BY THE SEA

164

"White walls offer a crisp contrast to mahogany floors and wood furnishings."

—*Waldo Fernandez*

165

"A good paint job is like having fabulous skin—no matter what you wear, you always look radiant."

—*Benjamin Noriega-Ortiz*

166

Paint walls to resemble something more costly like porphyry or horn veneer.

167

Create separate spaces without closing them off by defining them with folding screens, partial walls, or columns.

168

In a summer house, start with a neutral shell and add color with accessories.

169

"Give a living room architectural gravitas by adding an antique French limestone mantelpiece."

—Michael S. Smith

170

Paint the walls of a sitting room in a weekend house with an enchanting mural.

171

"Flank a gorgeous mural with built-in display shelves."

—Lee Bierly and Christopher Drake

172

"In a log cabin, accent a freestanding fireplace made of local river stones with a mantel of found timber."

—Vicente Wolf

173

"Embellish golden yellow walls with ethereal, hand-painted chinoiserie motifs in white."

—Mary Douglas Drysdale

174

"In a weekend house, use brilliant hues for a pure leisure look."

—William Diamond and Anthony Baratta

175

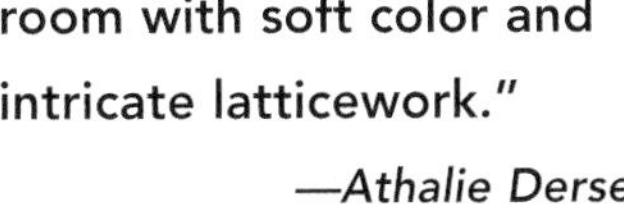

"Cover the walls of a sunroom with soft color and intricate latticework."

—Athalie Derse and Jeffrey Wyngarden

176

A fresh coat of paint can take decades off a tired room in an old home.

177

Flank a window in a library with floor-to-ceiling built-in bookshelves.

178

Create a greater sense of spaciousness between a dining room and living room by widening the opening between them.

179

"Create a sense of timeless beauty by resurfacing walls to give them an undulating, old-plaster look."

—Kerry Joyce

180

"Add character to a dining room with a simple but luxurious wainscoting."

—Lisa Jackson

181

Use semi- or high-gloss paint on millwork.

182

Using an oil-based paint on walls creates a creamy, lustrous look with depth.

183

"Latticework adds instant architecture where there is none and masks problems like uneven walls and cracking plaster."
— Anthony Baratta

184

Create an evocative atmosphere in a formal room with scenic sepia-painted canvas panels.

185

"Instead of predictable deep-toned hues in a library, opt for a neutral, restful, stone gray."

—Noel Jeffrey

Orientations

186

Pecky (naturally textured) cypress paneling lends warmth to a library.

187

"Create a comfortable ambience in a library by covering the walls with red linen."

—Thomas Pheasant

Section Two

Windows and Doors

188

"Take advantage of natural light by installing floor-to-ceiling windows and doors."

—William Diamond and Anthony Baratta

CHAGALL

189

"For rooms with views, avoid curtains with patterns."

—Scott Salvator

190

"Curtains can change a room from mediocre to amazing."

—Tim Clarke

191

Drapery fabric helps mute external noise.

192

"Milled shutters are functional and unobstrusive."

—Darryl Carter

193

"Give a room character with a Gothic window from an American country church."

—Kelly Harmon

194

Create instant character by recycling old conservatory doors in a new space.

195

"A shaped edge and contrasting trim gives extra polish to a crisp Roman shade."

—Greg Jordan

196

"For a classic modern look, try draperies or shades made of simple nubby linen the same color as the walls."

—Barbara Barry

Bring the outdoors in with massive windows and walls punctuated with glass doors.

198

"For something unique, try pierced Indian screens lacquered white and fitted into shutters."

—Andrew Fisher and Jeffry Weisman

199

"Delicately patterned, subtly trimmed window panels make a soaring room look formal yet relaxed."

—Bunny Williams

200

"Unlined cashmere curtains on a custom-made, hammered, flat steel pole with rectangular steel rings make a luxurious, classic modern statement."

—Hermes Mallea and Carey Maloney

201

"Add interest to an all-white room by installing a salvaged stained-glass church window."

—Gabriel de la Portilla

202

"Convert a tool shed into a guest house by adding French doors and windows."

—*Gabriel de la Portilla*

203

"Japanese shades are delicate and unobstrusive."

—*Diana Vinoly*

204

"For a nice inexpensive and simple window treatment, choose split bamboo blinds."

—*Tim Clarke*

205

"If done right, unlined taffeta curtains with deeply ruffled edges look like ball gowns."

—*Miles Redd*

206

"Balance the drama of a bay window with a substantial piece of furniture such as an expansive antique hutch."

—*Todd Romana*

207

Lend breezy informality to a cozy tea area with unlined, checked cotton curtains around the windows.

208

"Install glass walls to dissolve the boundaries between man-made space and nature."

—Graham Phillips

209

"Don't hesitate to replace several small windows with one large one if a room seems to call for it."

—Frank Babb Randolph

210

"Create a clean elegant look by combining flat Roman shades and simple drapes in unlined silk."

—Milly de Cabrol

211

"Line the curtains in different rooms with the same fabric so the house has a uniform look when viewed from the yard."

—Tim Clarke

212

"For a chic layered look, pair pencil-pleated silk draperies that pull up high with petite bamboo blinds underneath."

—Barclay Fryery

213

"Don't let the fact that you can't sew stop you from putting window treatments together."

—Whitney Stewart

214

In a space with a low ceiling, accentuate verticality by extending window frames up to the ceiling.

215

Add an element of surprise to streamlined draperies by lining them with ruby-red wool gabardine.

216

Mask an unfortunate view while allowing light to filter through by covering a window with a pleated sheer panel that remains drawn.

Section Three

Ceilings and Floors

217

Lend warmth to a large kitchen by painting stripes on the floor in olive drab and Creole red—traditional New Orleans colors.

218

"Ceilings coffered with a grid of wood take the curse off an expanse of bare planes."

—Jose Solis Betancourt

219

"Choose a virtually maintenance-free sisal rug for a woodsy retreat."

—Waldo Fernandez

220

Animate the floor of a small foyer with a checkerboard of oversize tiles.

221

"Treat a ceiling as a fifth wall by painting it with an allée of cream and beige trees."

—Eric Kohler

222

Install a mirrored ceiling over a crystal chandelier to expand a room and amplify light.

223

Strategically placed rough-hewn beams conjure up a sense of age.

224

Pickled floors give a space an ethereal quality.

225

Call attention to an interesting ceiling by leaving windows and floors bare or by covering them simply.

226

"Add comfort and interest to a windowless space by painting the ceiling with a mural or abstract pattern."

—Eric Cohler

227

"Create the perfect area rug by cutting and binding broadloom carpet to fit a space."

—Darryl Wilson

228

Water doesn't affect a rug made of a natural material like jute, which dries quickly.

229

"Add zest to a informal room by painting the floor with a design inspired by Pennsylvania Dutch hex symbols."

—Anthony Baratta and William Diamond

233

"Use salvaged French floor tiles in a garden room."

—Michael Smith

234

Choose a sisal with a cheery red border that picks up the color of cushions and curtains in a country kitchen.

235

Paint worn floorboards in a summer house a soft celadon green.

230

Ground a light-as-air, all-white room by staining a wood-plank floor very dark brown or black.

231

"A good Agra rug can elevate a room to the sublime."

—Todd Black

232

"A good rug can generate years of redecorating schemes."

—Kitty Hawks

236

"Add character to a formal living room with an exquisitely crafted coffered ceiling."

—Kerry Joyce

237

"Give a casual dining room patina by painting the floor with a faded checkerboard pattern."

—Lynn Morgan

Chapter Four

Lighting

238

Use gauze curtains to provide privacy yet admit light.

Nothing alters the mood of a room like light. To be comfortable as well as practical, every room needs just the right mix of overall ambient light, focused task illumination, and accent light.

Always include different kinds of fixtures to create an eye-pleasing composition of layered illumination. Introduce a soft overall glow with a central chandelier or ceiling fixture. Add focused light for various functions with a table lamp for reading, for example, or under-cabinet fixtures over a countertop in the kitchen. Then bring in energizing touches of sparkle with candlelight, sconces, or accent fixtures that highlight a work of art or sculpture. And put as many fixtures as possible on dimmers so you can customize light levels throughout the day.

Remember that natural light plays into the mix, too. Introduce more of it with larger or strategically placed windows; control it with scrim shades, shutters, or draperies.

239

Ever-changing light from outside plays on the hues in a room, altering them by the hour.

Section One

Natural Light

240

"Replacing an interior wall with a trellis of open wood shelves enables the flow of light between one space and another."

—Stephen Siegel

241

Let daylight permeate windowless rooms by adding clerestory panels above interior doorways and installing translucent glass in the interior doors.

242

"Paint your living room velvety midnight blue to create an exotic alchemy with natural light."

—Victoria Klein

243

To let in as much light as possible, install windows with steel frames—much thinner mullions can be fashioned from this material than from wood.

MILLERS ANTIQUES
MORRIS LOUIS

244

Surround a living room with walls of French windows and top it with a skylight to flood it with daylight.

245

"Wood shutters are great for controlling light."

—Orlando Diaz-Azcuy

246

"Flood a room with natural light by installing floor-to-ceiling windows and glass doors."

—Darryl Wilson

247

"Install a glass floor in a balcony to let natural light reach a room beneath it."

—Benjamin Noriega

BAUHAUS
BAUHAUS

248

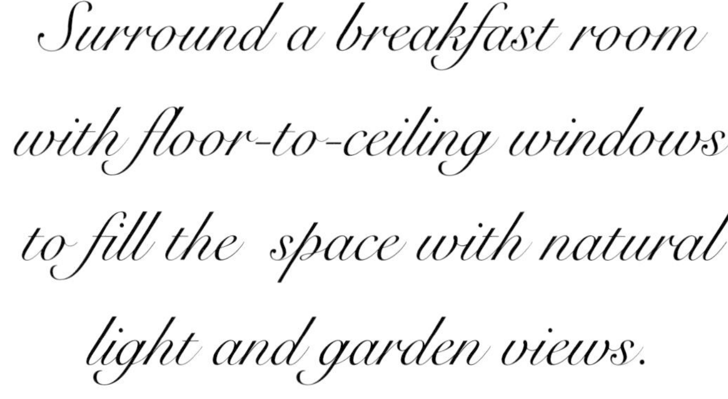

Surround a breakfast room with floor-to-ceiling windows to fill the space with natural light and garden views.

Section Two

Ambient, Task, and Accent Illumination

249

"Add interest as well as illumination with sculptural fixtures and shades."

—Benjamin Noriega-Ortiz

250

Hang a grandly sized chandelier in a living room with a high ceiling for drama and sparkle.

251

Use a Nordic trick for enhancing light by gilding a painted chair to reflect the sparkle of a crystal chandelier.

252

Chandeliers aren't just for the dining room—they also give a living room or a bedroom a warm glow at night."

—Scott Sanders

253

Make a fresh statement in a dining room by suspending a practical yet playful over-scale exterior lantern over the table.

254

Near a work area, include a mix of daylight and artificial illumination, ideally from a fabulous fixture such as a nine-armed Royere floor lamp.

255

"A few good mirrors and lamps will make the furniture look better and the space look bigger."

—David Netto

256

Over a kitchen island, install pendant fixtures with shades that glow with warm light.

257

"Even an inferior space, if thoughtfully lit, has the potential to be beautiful."

—Thomas Jayne

258

"In a very tall room, make a big statement with a massive chandelier."

—T. Keller Donovan

259

In a small space, use many sources of light—a minimum of two lights per wall—including sconces and picture lights as well as table and reading lamps.

260

"Always place dining room lanterns or chandeliers over the center of the table and remember that from the table top to the bottom of the fixture there should be no less than thirty to thirty-six inches."

—T. Keller Donovan

261

Provide task light for countertops in a kitchen with incandescent strip lights discreetly hidden beneath overhead cabinets.

262

Forgo recessed lighting and use decorative fixtures instead.

263

"Sconces should be placed sixty-eight inches from the floor to the electrical box."

—T. Keller Donovan

264

In a massive room, suspend three chandeliers rather than just one for ambient illumination, include a variety of table and floor lamps for task light, and use plenty of candles for sparkle.

Section Three

Controlling Light

265

Hang linen and wool panels from a traverse curtain rod suspended along a ceiling beam to serve as both a room divider and a scrim that filters light.

Edward Weston
KARL LAGERFELD off the record

266

Filter light with layered window treatments such as roll-up matchstick blinds and floor-length draperies.

267

Create a warm glow at a party by applying amber gels over light bulbs.

268

Put all lighting on dimmers so you can set different moods.

269

"In a master bedroom, cover windows with Roman shades that can be handily controlled from the bed."

—Noel Jeffrey

270

Cover a picture window with sheer wool panels that permit views while diffusing light by day and provide privacy in the evening.

271

Layer lighting in a dining room with a dimmable chandelier, sconces to accent a mantel or sideboard, and candles to create shimmer on the table.

272

Flank a mirror with sconces and cover them with frosted glass shades for optimal, diffused illumination.

273

Amplify the light in a large room by positioning a mirror over a mantel to reflect the light of a crystal chandelier.

274

In the tropics, cover living room windows with iridescent raw silk drapes that control sunlight and reflect it softly at the same time.

Chapter Five

Creating Family Friendly Spaces

Top upholstered seating with kid-friendly denim slipcovers.

If you've got kids or pets, or if family and friends visit regularly, make them feel at ease with an ample supply of creature comforts such as oversize ottomans, comfy cushions, and daybeds. Keep maintenance simple by choosing durable, easy-care, or inexpensive materials and furnishings like denim slipcovers, sisal carpets, and metal barstools.

Merge form with function by creating dual-purpose spaces, for instance, a guest room that doubles as a home office, or by including multi-functional furniture, like benches that include storage. And build in convenience and style with cabinets or shelves with flip-down doors that hide TV, stereos, and toys.

276

"Placing a flat-panel TV opposite a sofa in an unobstrusive way accommodates family activities in a sleek living room."

—Eve Robinson

Section One

Defining Comfort Zones

277

Pile an antique wicker sofa with a mélange of soft pillows.

278

"Carve out a special spot for a pet in the mud-room."

—Tim Clarke

279

For a room that can absorb dogs and children, establish a comfort level without pretension.

280

"Concentrate on lots of comfortable seating in a living room so it can be a real hangout instead of a ceremonial space used only at big cocktail parties."

—David Netto

The Golden Age of Dutch Art
John James Audubon

281

"Convert the rooftop servants' quarters of a turn-of-the-century home into a cozy office."

—Anne Marie

282

"Give soul to a modern room with a Buddha statue from Thailand."

—Benjamin Noriega-Ortiz

283

"In an older home, preserve character by resisting the trend to combine the family room and kitchen."

—Tim Clarke

284

"Create a 'home away from home' office by installing an Aeron chair, a Hollywood white-lacquered baroque desk, and a cushioned window-seat in a room surrounded by windows."

—Matthew White

285

In a beach house, create a napping nook fitted with a drawer for holding blankets.

286

"Remove items (such as dog biscuits or dishwashing powder) that are normally stowed in a kitchen or utility room from their ugly packages and put them in big decorative glass jars instead."

—Jackie Terrell

287

"A lot of laundry rooms don't have windows, so combat the lack of a view with artwork that suggests the outdoors."

—Jackie Terrell

288

Up the comfort quotient in a living room by incorporating plenty of upholstered sofas and chairs while steering away from strong color.

289

"Use overscale, slipcovered furniture in a family room for a soft, casual look."

—Gary McBournie

"Include a mix of modern and traditional furnishings and accessories to create rooms that look smart, up-to-date, old-fashioned, and cozy all at the same time."

—Tom Scheerer

291

Increase the cheer factor in a kitchen by adding a hand-painted Bavarian corner bench and table.

Section Two

Easy-Care Ideas

292

"Choose no-fuss, fine-lined furnishings."

—Jose Solis Betancourt

293

"A table topped with a thick slab of marble set on a rug-free marble floor adds up to a low-maintenance dining room."

—Celia Cabral

294

"Upholster a sofa in easy-to-maintain ultraleather—especially if you have a pet."

—Benjamin Noriega-Ortiz

295

Make wash-and-wear slipcovers in a weekend house from three-dollar-a-yard curtain-lining fabric.

296

Opt for natural materials and fibers for a casual, simple look.

297

"Dress down a tropical winter home with cotton slipcovers and sisal carpets."

—Robin Bell Shafer

298

Install low-maintenance sandblasted travertine floors in a weekend house.

299

"Eschew fancy furnishings and choose good quality modern pieces mixed with a few antiques for a soft, cozy atmosphere."

—Celia Cabral Domenech

300

"If no piece of furniture is off-limits to your pets, cover everything in plain, inexpensive, practically indestructible cotton duck slipcovers—and buy an extra bolt in case of emergencies."

—Robin Bell Shafer

301

Let an ottoman—with a washable slipcover—substitute for a hard-edged coffee table in front of the TV in a family room.

302

"Wash new fabric before turning it into slipcovers so it feels soft."

—Helen Ballard Weeks

Section Three

Mixing Form with Function

303

Craft a built-in niche for a large screen television.

SONY

304

Hide a stereo system and TV behind large prints in frames that swing open and shut.

305

Integrate the projector and audio-visual elements of an entertainment system into a custom shelf.

306

Hide speakers in built-in niches covered with screens painted to match walls.

307

Let a guest room double as a comfortable home office by installing a daybed; add a built-in wall unit that converts to a desk by day and conceals machines like a fax or printer at night.

308

For a more simple, low-maintenance take on eighteenth-century formality, decorate with painted Gustavian furniture.

309

Conceal a television and stereo equipment in neat, built-in cabinets.

310

"Put a corkboard on one half of a side-by-side refrigerator and a blackboard on the other—the fridge is a great place for a family to touch base."

—Peter Dunham

311

"Stow a TV inside a turn-of-the-century Chinese cupboard."

—Tom Scheerer

312

"Choose furniture that's substantial without being stodgy."

—David Netto

Over the Line
ANDY GOLDSWORTHY
MAHARAJAS' JEWELS
THE VENDOME PRESS

313

A laundry room can be both functional and fun: choose fresh citrus accents to contrast with clean white counters and shelves.

314

"Hide the washer and dryer in a laundry area behind sliding curtains mounted beneath a countertop, and add a big attractive utility table."

—Jackie Terrell

315

"Craft a banquette with built-in dog beds."

—Chris Madden

316

Add warmth and function to a contemporary kitchen by using an old oak table as an island.

317

Add comfort and cheer to a family kitchen by painting walls a bright sunny color.

318

Anchor a large kitchen with a red center worktable that's built in but doesn't look like it is—include integrated outlets and drawers on both sides.

TABASCO

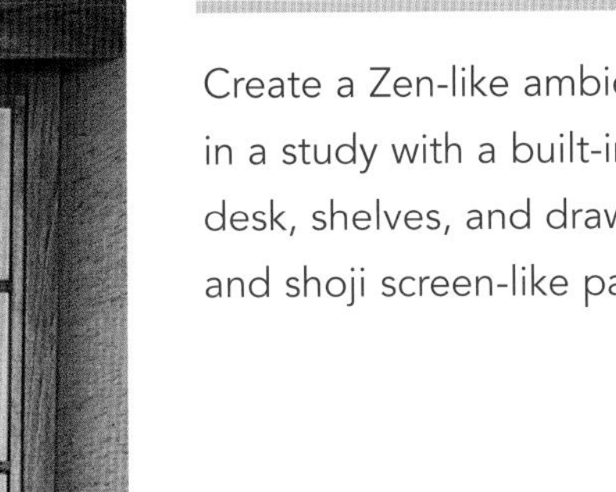

319

Create a Zen-like ambience in a study with a built-in desk, shelves, and drawers and shoji screen-like panels.

320

"Use the space on either side of a hearth to store a television and firewood."

—Graham Phillips

Chapter Six

Beautiful, Functional Kitchens and Baths

Halogen is a great light source because it is so flattering to different colors and finishes in a kitchen.

Whether it's small or large, traditional or modern, chances are your kitchen is the heart of your home. No longer just the place where meals are prepared, the kitchen has become command central—where children gather, homework gets done, the news is watched, and bills are paid. Let it serve your family, then, by renovating it if necessary, carefully adapting its layout to suit your needs, and adding materials and appliances that are as hardworking as they are pleasing to the eye.

Bathrooms, on the other hand, are places to get away from it all. So make sure yours includes elements that soothe the senses. Turn a tiny powder room into a jewel-like sanctuary by splurging on gorgeous fixtures, or convert a master bath into a spa-like retreat by covering its floors and surrounding its walls with polished marble. A little luxury goes a long way.

322

Place the tub right next to a window in a bath that has an ocean view.

Section One

Devising a Plan and Defining Style

323

Let an antique farm table double as a kitchen island.

324

"In a contemporary kitchen, consider using materials like steel, stone, concrete, and glass for their durability."

—Page Goolrick

325

Ceiling height can vary in a room, so be sure to measure it in three separate places to ensure that everything fits.

326

Place the dishwasher next to the sink to avoid dripping on the floor.

327

"Make a strong style statement by working with a theme such as Gothic Revival and playing it up to the hilt."

—William Diamond and Anthony Baratta

328

"Combine modern conveniences with old-world charm."

—Jose Solis Betancourt

329

Fit out a custom kitchen island with a sink or two.

330

Start the planning process as early as possible to give your designer the flexibility to modify room size and window locations and work with connecting areas like entries, mudrooms, or pantries.

331

Expect the cost of a new kitchen to be between 10 and 20 percent of the value of the house.

332

Hide the bottle storage area of a pantry bar with curtains.

333

"Pep up a corner in a contemporary kitchen with modernist accessories—say a George Nelson light fixture, Eero Saarinan table, and Arne Jacobsen chairs."

—Neil Korpinen and Rick Erikson

334

"Install a window seat between a family room and kitchen to both separate and connect them."

—Tim Clarke

335

Add a pantry for extra storage.

336

It's next to impossible to match wood cabinets and wood floors—so go for tones that harmonize in pleasing contrast.

337

"Don't leave windows bare in a kitchen."

—*Peter Dunham*

338

"Matchstick shades diffuse light and give a sense of privacy; linen curtains are very cheerful and easily washed."

—*Peter Dunham*

339

"Use old-fashioned materials to make a kitchen feel more welcoming."

—*Jackie Terrell*

340

"A kitchen is usually all traditional or all modern, but it's much more interesting to incorporate elements of both."

—Michael Smith

341

"Brighten pale walls with artwork."

—Michael Smith

342

Make a hardworking butcher block island look like a painted farmhouse table by adding turned legs.

343

Create a sense of luxury in a master bath by including a freestanding tub carved from a single piece of Carrara marble.

344

Add a touch of luxury to a small bath with a silk Roman shade and marble flooring.

Section Two

Appliances and Cabinets

345

"Give cabinets presence with crown molding and fluted corners topped with rosettes."

—Barbara Bell

349

Space permitting, design lower cabinets layouts with an angled return at one end to allow an extra prep area.

350

Use glass-fronted cabinets for displaying pretty pottery collections.

351

"Install foot pedals in an island to operate a faucet."

—Tim Clarke

352

"No kitchen should be designed without under-cabinet lighting."

—Mick Di Giulio

346

"In a country kitchen, strip cabinets of glass panes and add chicken wire in their place."

—Kelly Harmon

347

An eighteen-inch-wide dishwasher is adequate for a family of three.

348

"Standard overhead cabinetry is the first way to date a house."

—Bobbie McAlpine

353

"Glass-fronted cabinets show off dishes and make a small kitchen feel bigger rather than boxed in."

—Stephen Siegel

354

For a big family kitchen, install a pair of matching refrigerators.

355

"A tall pantry and open shelves are timeless."

—Bobbie McAlpine

356

Brighten a narrow kitchen by adding lights inside glass-fronted cabinets and installing glass shelves.

357

"A major downside to a side-by-side refrigerator is that the freezer is often too narrow for a lot of items like frozen pizzas and sheet cakes."

—Mick Di Giulio

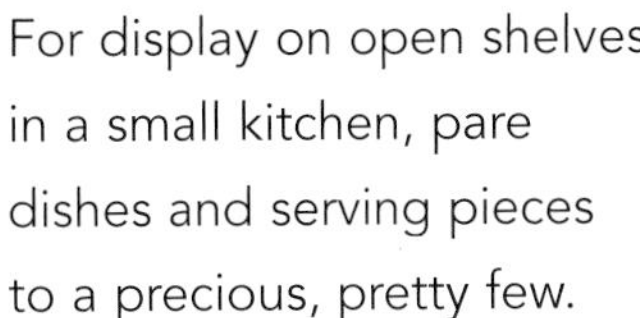

358

For display on open shelves in a small kitchen, pare dishes and serving pieces to a precious, pretty few.

359

"In a small kitchen, extend cabinets into an adjoining room to provide more storage space."

—Jay Jeffers

360

Give undistinguished cabinets a budget-wise facelift with a coat of fresh white paint and some low-cost, handpainted knobs from a stylish retailer.

361

If you have limited floor space, choose a side-by-side refrigerator that's only twenty-four inches deep.

362

"Build drama into a bathroom with iconic columns and a step-up tub."

——Gary McBournie

363

"Store bath towels, soaps, and toiletries on pretty two- or three-tier antique painted tables."

—Keith Irvine

364

"The ideal kitchen has a high shelf around the perimeter for displaying china."

—Keith Irvine

365

To add visual interest, custom-dye concrete counters to bring out the material's natural variations.

366

"Keep toiletries in a full-height medicine cabinet."

—Celeste Cooper

367

"If you're a busy couple, but you have the luxury of a large, wonderful bathroom, you can just putter along there and talk and connect with your spouse."

—William Hodgins

368

"Front cabinets with glass the color of a Perrier bottle."

—Alison Spear

369

Create a niche with glass shelves at the head of the tub for stowing neatly folded towels.

370

Define a bathroom with a Mediterranean theme by covering its wall with Moorish tiles.

371

Roll and store bath towels in a niche below a heated towel rack.

Section Three

Fixtures, Fittings, and Finishes

372

"Create a focal point with a Provencal-style wrought-iron pot rack."

—Mary Douglas Drysdale

BREAD
SALT

373

Add an unusual note to a straightforward kitchen by installing a whimsical chandelier.

374

"An antique pot rack provides both a sculptural and practical touch."

—Tim Clarke

375

If you're an avid cook, consider an extra-deep sink to handle large pots.

376

"If you use softer stones like limestone and marble as countertops, remember that they will etch and absorb stains and marks—but you can minimize marks by coating them with a proper nontoxic sealer."

—Mick Di Giulio

380

Granite is a beautiful counter surface, but it's also porous and can stain—even when sealed.

381

A wood floor in the kitchen is easy on the feet.

382

One of the best ways to brighten a kitchen is by incorporating reflected ceiling lighting instead of using only recessed cans or other downlights.

383

Cup-pull handles on drawers subtly contribute to a vintage aura.

377

"To give a wood floor some sheen, finish it with a coat of semigloss sandwiched between two coats of satin polyurethane."

—Stephen Siegel

378

"For task light in kitchens, use incandescent strip lights in twelve-inch segments, which are easier to install and don't burn out as frequently as longer lights."

—Stephen Siegel

379

Make sure your kitchen rug has a rubber backing to prevent slippage.

384

"Enliven a kitchen with hand-stamped floor tiles."

—*Peter Dunham*

385

"Add cozy charm to kitchen cabinets by lining their doors with block-printed Indian fabric."

—Peter Dunham

386

Add grace notes to cabinets with colored glass insets and knobs that match the colors of a tiled backsplash.

387

"Install countertops made of soapstone because it bashes up a lot and develops wonderful flaws the more it's used."

—Peter Dunham

388

To give marble countertops a softer look, make sure they're honed rather than polished.

389

"Stone floors can be hard to stand on for long periods, and can feel cold to bare feet if not heated."

—Mick Di Giulio

390

To create a spa-like bath, line the tub with marble.

391

"Paint the outside of an antique tub in bands of color that complement the window treatments."

—William Holloway

392

"Add zest to a guest bathroom by painting a claw-foot tub red."

—Kathryn M. Ireland

393

Use honed marble tiles for a floor with a stony, user-friendly scratch-proof finish.

394

"Complement a ceramic or cast-iron tub with traditional English fixtures and fittings."

—Kelly Wearstler

395

"Use a tile enhancer on tumbled stone to bring out color and eliminate chalkiness (apply with a brush after the stone is set in grout)."

—Barbara Bell

396

Limit the number of dramatic materials in a room.

397

If you must have the color of the moment, limit it to wall paint so you can repaint when you tire of it.

398

A mirrored transom over a short window gives it the illusion of having more height.

399

Always put lighting on dimmers so you can control the atmosphere.

400

"Bring visual richness to a monochromatic bath by using a veined Carrarra marble countertop, a pearly mosaic floor, and gleaming silver-plated sink and shower fittings."

—Thomas O'Brien

Chapter Seven

Bedroom Basics

401

An upholstered headboard brings a sophisticated look to a room.

Your bedroom is your refuge—the place in which you wind down at night and wake up at daybreak. As such, it should envelop you with colors, textures, furnishings, and fabrics that nourish your body and your soul. The bed sets the tone for the whole room, so create a romantic place to dream in with layers of luscious bed linens, a Zen-like sanctuary with an oversize platform bed, or a luxurious retreat with a regal silk canopy.

Include other elements of comfort, too—wall-to-wall carpet, an antique night stand, an overstuffed chair and ottoman, a reading lamp, draperies that provide privacy, a television armoire that shuts out technology, candles that create ambience. Remember that guests value these things as well.

402

For a soothing effect in a bedroom, use calm slate-blue and ivory tones on the walls, windows, and floor.

MADE IN TEXAS
SOUTH CAROLINA A History

Section One

Dressing the Bed

403

Add an extra note of comfort to a guest room by upholstering a sleigh bed.

404

Keep it simple—but fun—in a guest room.

405

"Suspend do-it-yourself canopies from bamboo rods over twin beds in a guest room."

—Jean-Louis Deniot

406

"Make a pretty bolster using the fabric of an antique kimono."

—Victoria Klein

407

Layer blue-and-white striped linens in the bedroom of a summer house.

408

"Give a modern kick to a bedroom by upholstering a headboard in a solid-colored fabric and keeping trim to a minimum."

—Tom Scheerer

409

"Fashion a do-it-yourself canopy by Velcroing a valance made from old curtains onto a salvaged piece of brass."

—Robin Bell Shafer

410

Add glamour to a four-poster bed by topping it with a custom-made canopy.

411

Make a standard ceiling seem higher by surrounding the bed with a tall, tailored canopy.

412

"Add interest to a no-poster bed by surrounding it with curtains made from hand-blocked Indian fabric hung on brass rails suspended from the ceiling."

—John Dransfield and Geoffrey Ross

413

"I love strong colors and use them everywhere; my bed is draped in red, and it's big enough for the whole family on Sunday morning."

—Kathryn Ireland

414

Play up the height of a tall room by topping twin beds with awning-like canopies suspended from the ceiling.

415

Bring a sophisticated look to a room with an upholstered headboard.

416

Upholster a headboard in a fabric that matches the wallpaper.

417

"Cover a Gustavian bed with a regal canopy."

—Marianne von Kantzow

Section Two

Furnishings and Creature Comforts

418

"Use portieres to section off a windowed sitting area from the bed."

—Jose Solis Betancourt

419

"Use machine-washable fabrics in a child's room."
—Katie Ridder

420

Cozy up a room by adding doors fitted with metal mesh to open shelves.

421

"Matching night stands aren't always necessary."
—Frank DelleDonne

422

"Marry masculine and feminine elements."
—Mary McDonald

423

"Provide your children with simple, good-looking storage units, such as multidrawered cabinets for Tinkertoys, blocks, and the like."
—Katie Ridder

424

Create a place for reading and writing in a bedroom.

425

Fashion a throw pillow from vintage fabric.

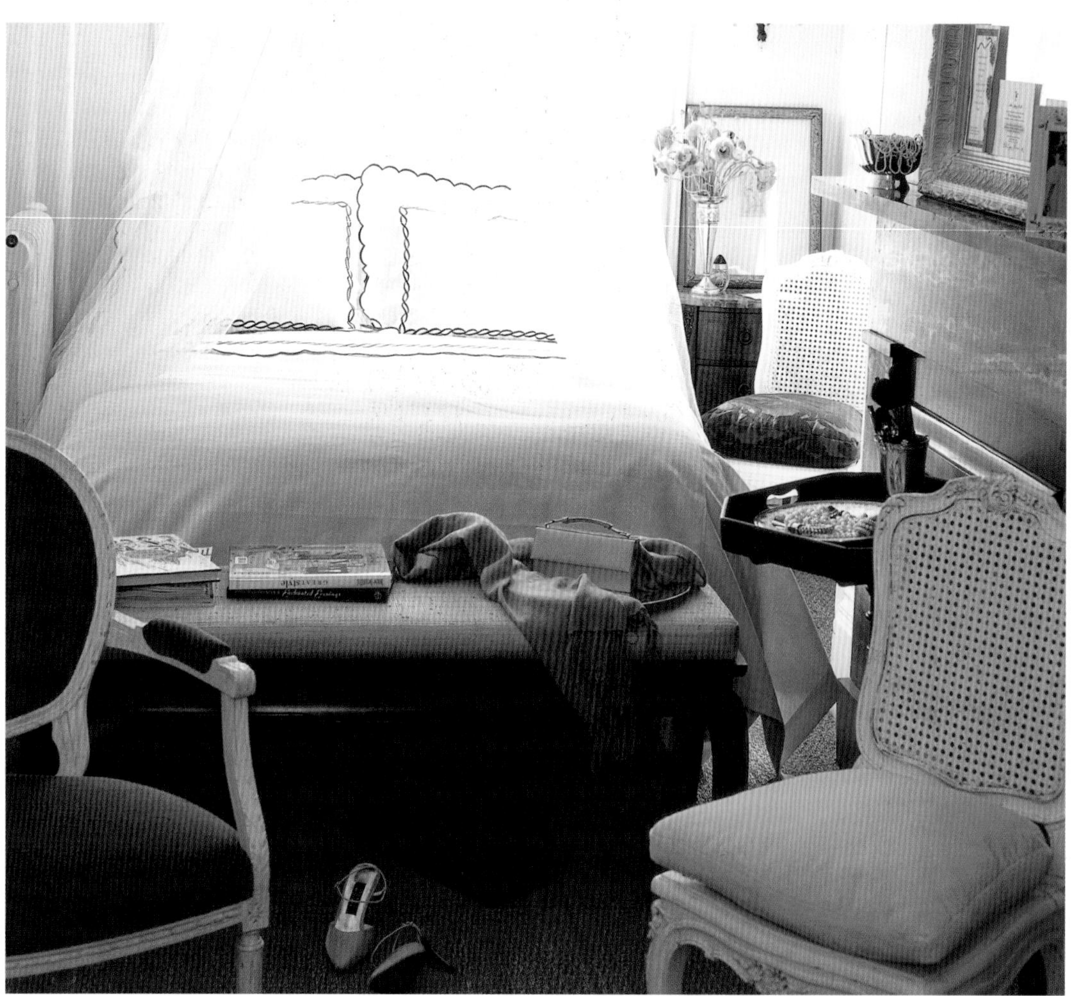

426

"Give an all-white bedroom punches of color by covering chair seats with fabrics in plum, lemon, and mango hues."

—Mary Taylor McGee

428

"Reupholster an antique armchair and ottoman and add them to the corner of a bedroom for a great place to curl up and read a book."

—*Chris Madden*

427

Include interesting furnishings, a collection of books, and tea things in a guest room to keep visitors content until you wake up.

429

Convert a pair of seventeenth-century Japanese altar candleholders into bedside lamps.

430

"Look at traditional elements in fresh ways."

—Barclay Butera

431

"Turn an antique trunk into a bedside table."

—Brad Blair

432

An antique wrought-iron bed adds character to a spartan guest room.

433

"Mixing materials and periods makes you really appreciate the texture and color of each object."

—Frank DelleDonne

434

Create serenity in a bedroom with materials, bedding, and accents in various shades of white.

435

"Stow blankets in an antique Spanish chest at the foot of a bed."

—Martyn Lawrence-Bullard

436

Keep a light throw at the foot of a bed in a guest room and store extra blankets in the closet.

437

An armchair next to a swing-arm lamp provides an alternative to reading in bed.

Section Three

Walls, Windows, Ceilings, and Floors

438

"Create an atmosphere of serenity by hanging a panel of plain linen against the wall behind your headboard."

—Holly Hunt

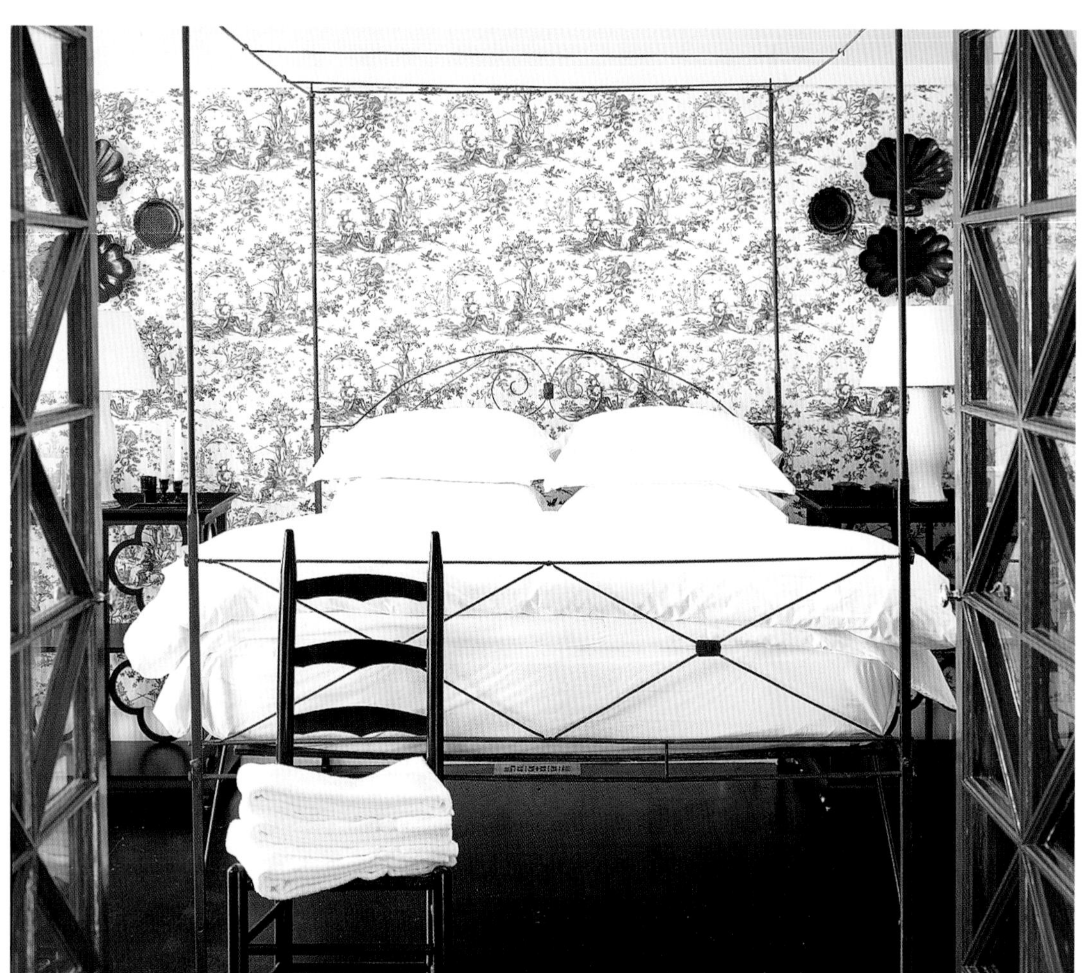

439

"Use a cavalcade of pattern in a large bedroom."

—Anthony Baratta and William Diamond

440

"Paint the walls of a young girl's bedroom with stripes in two pale shades of pink."

—Tim Clarke

441

Add detail to a high, open space by placing decorative beams on the ceiling.

442

"If we use a printed toile in a room, that's all you'll find—no checks, no stripes—we're great believers in holding back."

—Lee Bierly and Christopher Drake

443

For richness and warmth, cover a bedroom wall with velvet.

444

"Consider finishes such as Venetian plaster, upholstered walls, or leather floors."

—Antonia Hutt

445

Install tasseled valances over windows curtained in a printed linen.

446

"Layer a bedroom in a sunny clime with a spectrum of floral hues."

—William Diamond and Anthony Baratta

447

"A guest room should have its own completely different look."

—*T. Keller Donovan*

448

"Cover an inset behind the bed with linen and accent the walls with hand-stenciled borders."

—*Anthony Baratta and William Diamond*

449

Dress the windows in a girl's room with sheer white swags trimmed with ball fringe.

450

"Make a bedroom cozy by covering walls with a period floral wallpaper, but keep it from looking grannyish by keeping the rest of the elements, including furniture and window treatments, streamlined."

—*Rita Konig*

451

"Use chocolate brown walls as a backdrop for pale prints surrounded by pretty pink mats."

—*Mary McDonald*

452

Use a monochromatic scheme in a bedroom to allow the shape of furniture to stand out.

453

If your room has northern exposure, paint it a lively pink or periwinkle blue.

454

"For a sense of romance in a master bedroom, create a serene backdrop of wallpaper—hand-stenciled in Italy—to set off a mix of formal yet deeply comfortable furnishings."

—Michael S. Smith

455

Add a pretty personal touch by handpainting or stenciling garlands on the walls.

456

"A quiet, creamy background provides serenity."

—Chris Madden

457

Create a soothing yet playful ambience by painting the walls chocolate brown and making curtains from a batik-style cotton print fabric.

458

Consider using materials like linen and ticking stripes, seagrass floor covering, and chocolate brown paint favored by the late masterful designer Billy Baldwin.

Chapter Eight

Solutions for Small Spaces

459

Curtains that run floor to ceiling and wall to wall transform ordinary windows into elegant focal points.

Small rooms can be beautiful—especially when you decorate them using a few tricks of the trade. Begin by making a list of the functions you want the room to serve, then employ space-expanding techniques and choose furnishings that support them.

You can fool the eye with mirrors, for example, which reflect and amplify light and create the illusion of twice as much space. Or you can use moldings or paint techniques to create perspectives that keep you from feeling closed in.

Furnishing small spaces involves one part common sense, one part counter-intuition. Do, for example, incorporate multipurpose pieces such as an ottoman that does triple-duty as a coffee table, a seating element, and a storage spot for books or blankets. But don't include undersize chairs or rugs, which make a diminutive space seem even smaller.

460

Consider the placement of mirrored walls or hanging or leaning mirrors carefully—there should be a focal point such as artwork placed opposite so they reflect something interesting.

Section One

Furnish Wisely

461

"To maximize seating in a small study, include a custom-designed L-shaped sofa."

—Todd Romana

462

A den or living room can double as a guest room when you add a daybed.

463

"Small spaces must be intentionally decorated because if they aren't, they make you feel like you're living in a shoe box."

—Jean-Louis Deniot

464

Give a dual-purpose daybed a crisp, non-bed-roomy look by upholstering it in a palette of black and white plus one other color and covering pillows or cushions with striped fabric.

465

Before you design your small space, make a list of all the functions you need performed in the room—then shop for furnishings that can service several of them.

466

Use furniture made of metal, mirror, or Plexiglass.

467

Gravitate toward large-scale furniture and accessories. Use an upholstered screen with a different fabric on each side to divide your space. Make one side a giant memento board: tack on grosgrain ribbon in a crisscrossing lattice pattern and tuck in cards or photos.

468

Add drama to a small entrance hall by hanging a gilded sunburst mirror over a console.

469

Stick to furnishings with strong shapes.

470

"Because the eye notices everything in a small space, you can't have mediocre things—instead decorate with good furniture and beautiful little engravings and paintings."

—Jean-Louis Deniot

471

Show some leg. Use unskirted furniture to give the illusion of depth; skirted furniture can close off a room.

472

"Create perspectives so you don't feel closed in."

—Jean-Louis Deniot

473

Squeeze a few more chairs around a pedestal table—and choose a table with a convenient leaf.

474

"Opt for furniture with exposed wood frames to allow tiny rooms to breathe."

—Gabriel de la Portilla

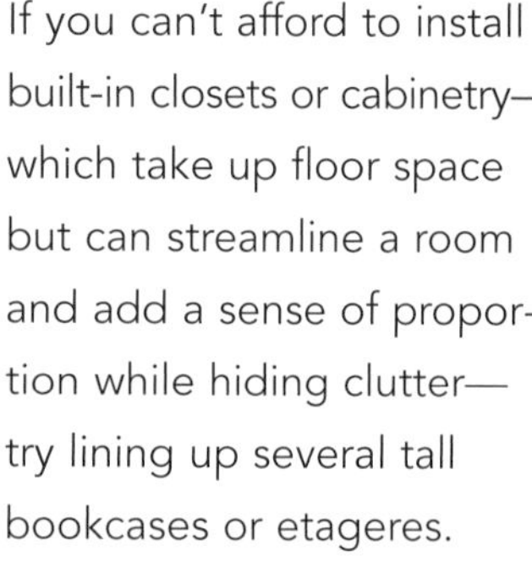

475

"Use a large, glass-topped, steel-framed coffee table to add a lot of surface but very little visual weight to a small living room."

—Gabriel de la Portilla

476

To make a one-room apartment feel much bigger, create different zones for different functions.

477

Put a bed on casters so you can roll it out from the wall and change the sheets more easily.

478

If you can't afford to install built-in closets or cabinetry—which take up floor space but can streamline a room and add a sense of proportion while hiding clutter—try lining up several tall bookcases or etageres.

479

"Choose chairs that are light and leggy."

—Jean-Louis Deniot

480

"Don't light the ceiling or you'll feel it's on your head."

—Jean-Louis Deniot

481

Be whimsical with the decor in a pied-a-terre.

482

Use fabric as a room divider—it's an inexpensive way to change the mood of a space and works especially well in studios and lofts.

483

Think big! In addition to overscale furniture, try wall-to-wall carpeting to unify a space, or no carpet at all.

484

Undersize rugs only make a room look smaller.

485

Use lampshades that concentrate the light to give the impression that the space is larger.

Section Two

Architectural Elements, Built-Ins, and Space-Saving Storage Solutions

486

Conceal clutter with a pretty table skirt.

487

Forget cluttered kitchen storage—hang your pots.

488

Put your walls to work and hang everything they can support: bedside lighting, ledges to display artwork, pots and pans.

489

Hide storage—hang a curtain across a wall.

490

Install a faux fireplace to hide a radiator behind real logs and become a focal point.

491

To add height to a room with low ceilings, install crown moldings, which allow the eye to rest before moving up again, giving the illusion of height.

492

Choose dual-purpose furniture like cocktail tables that elevate to dining-table height, or pieces that roll, stack, and store.

493

Pilasters will add a classical, built-in touch to ready-made bookshelves.

494

"Open up a room with a low ceiling by taking out the floor above, and reinforcing the places where joists were removed with tie rods."

—Lee Bierly and Christopher Drake

495

Use moldings to provide rhythm and verticality.

496

"In a dining room that doubles as an office, create a custom credenza that serves as both a desk and a sideboard (with drawers that are sized for table linens as well as files)."

—Tony Cantalini

497

Don't overdress your windows—let them breathe and admit maximum light into the room.

498

Move a door if necessary to borrow light and a view from a window in an adjacent room.

499

Artful arrangements of books and bibelots can greatly contribute to an interior, but messy details like stereo wires and piles of junk mail can wreak havoc in a small space.

500

Step out the lower section of floor-to-ceiling shelves so it can also serve as a bar or buffet.

Section Three

Fool-the-Eye Tricks with Color, Texture, and Pattern

501

"Keep the color scheme simple in a small space—stick to two or three colors, using one mainly as the punctuation."

—T. Keller Donovan

Lewis Grizzard
THE LAST GIRLS
SEVEN PROMISES
PROMISE KEEPER
ITALY
GREAT BRITAIN
FRANCE
CALIFORNIA
LONDON
The Hotel New Hampshire

Reflective surfaces create the illusion of depth.

503

A transparent shower curtain makes a small bathroom look larger.

504

"Use pattern sparingly—too much will make your room look like a television text pattern."

—Eric Cohler

505

"Paint the walls of a small space with chocolate brown semigloss and add zest with accents in a bright hue such as Hermes-box orange."

—Ned Marshall.

506

"Try using texture instead of pattern for added interest."

—Eric Cohler

507

"Paint the whole room, including the floor, white so that everything recedes and you can't tell where the floor begins and where it ends."

—T. Keller Donovan

508

A mirror-covered wall amplifies light from a window to make a small room brighter.

509

"Apply moldings to doors and mount pictures on them so that they blend in with walls."

—Jean-Louis Deniot

510

Light-colored floors can contribute to the semblance of ample space, especially when combined with dark, lacquered walls.

511

Oversize paintings or photographs open up rooms, creating a vista or second window—especially if there is no view.

512

"Add a focal piece like a faux tortoiseshell chest of drawers for a touch of glamour—you always need that certain something to make a room pop."

—Elizabeth Orenstein.

513

Tortoiseshell blinds can mask an unattractive view yet still let in light.

514

Install simple curtains hung as close to the ceiling as possible, or a crisp Roman shade with a contrasting border.

515

Experiment with unusual colors and reflective surfaces to make walls disappear.

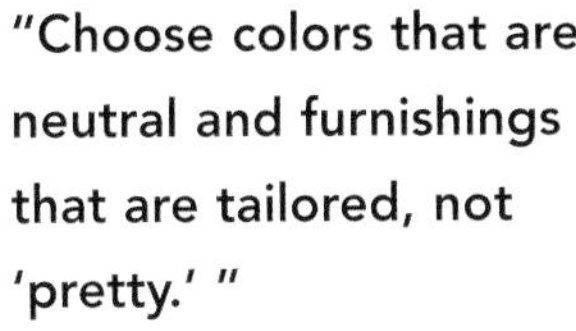

516

"Choose colors that are neutral and furnishings that are tailored, not 'pretty.' "

—Elizabeth Orenstein.

517

Banish fussy window treatments.

518

Painting low ceilings with semigloss paint will make them seem higher.

519

Use lamps, sconces, and ceiling fixtures to layer lighting and create gradations of visual texture.

520

"Shimmery dark walls give the illusion of space—you can't see the corners and you ignore that they are actually in close."

—Ned Marshall

Chapter Nine

Art and Accessories

521

Make a bold impression by framing a collection of graphic elements like arrowheads and amassing the frames along a single wall.

Instead of looking at works of art or cherished collectibles as finishing touches to a room, why not view them as starting points? Turn a collection of vibrant Napoli lettuceware into a focal point by displaying it in a massive breakfront and rely on its colors to influence the palette of the room. Or let a collection of fine art stand out by eliminating all else but the bare essentials.

Even humble objects like wire baskets or watercolors done by children gain stature—and create character—when you group or display them conscientiously. Use color as the common thread that ties together a disparate collection of teacups. Or create a striking composition by juxtaposing a modern photograph with a weathered antique table. The element of surprise adds energy.

522

"Cluster a collection of rare antique plates on a sideboard."

—Keith Irvine

Section One

Hanging and Showcasing Art

523

"Hanging photographs at eye level gives them greater impact."

—*Eve Robinson*

524

"Compensate for a lack of view by hanging a large, moody landscape painting to create a de facto window."

—Eric Cohler

525

Pictures should be grouped together to create mass.

526

"Turn a small entrance vestibule into an exclamation point by layering it floor to ceiling with abstract paintings."

—Eric Cohler

527

"In a hallway, where you are always standing as opposed to sitting, hang pictures higher."

—T. Keller Donovan

528

Surmount a low dresser with a large mirror flanked by a quartet of prints.

529

In a summer house, frame a map of the area to create instant art—and an easy reference for weekend guests.

530

Instead of hanging a large piece of framed art, set it on the floor and lean it against a wall.

531

Strong art needs the environment of a strong house.

532

"Embrace eclectic contradictions: try hanging an abstract work of art over a seventeenth-century Italian coffer or topping a nineteenth-century carved wood console with a contemporary sculpture."

—Dan Carithers

533

Hang a contemporary painting in a room full of antiques.

534

Frame a pair of graphic quilts and hang them on a tall wall like paintings.

Kandinsky
Vasily Kandinsky A Colorful Life
KANDINSKY
Catalogue Raisonné of the Oil-Paintings
Sotheby

535

If your walls are full and you've got a new print, painting, drawing, or watercolor you simply must display, lean it on a seldom used chair.

536

"Display a valuable piece of art on a custom-made easel."

—John Oetgen

537

"Create a striking juxtaposition by hanging a modern photograph above a gnarled wood table."

—Mariette Himes Gomez

538

"If you prefer not to measure, hang a collection of flea-market engravings haphazardly."

—Kathryn Ireland

539

Make a strong statement with a collection of tiny drawings by surrounding them with overscale mats and sleek frames and hanging them in a single column from floor to ceiling.

540

"If your frames are a hodgepodge of styles and sizes, painting them one color gives your room a sense of order."

—T. Keller Donovan

541

Create a special illuminated niche in which to display a sculpture or prized object.

542

Tack or tape a collection of unframed watercolors to a wall in a summer house.

543

Flank a doorway with a grouping of engravings.

544

Create a lovely still life by arranging several cloisonné vessels next to a small bronze sculpture on an antique table.

545

"Everything looks more important if it's surrounded with at least a two-inch border of matting."

—T. Keller Donovan

Section Two

Displaying Collectibles

546

"Create a still life with selected objects from your collections."

—Scott Salvator

547

Show off a collection of pretty plates on built-in shelves in an eat-in kitchen.

548

Even the most humble object—a wire basket, a birdcage, a cider jug—looks interesting if you collect several and display them together.

549

Lend importance to a pair of vases by mounting them on pedestals flanking a door.

550

"Display a collection of blue-and-white plates from many countries and periods on plate rails under the eaves of a guest room."

—Nannette Brown

551

Complement a collection of blue-and-white export china with slipcovers and fabrics in the same hues.

552

Set off a collection of earthy-hued pottery in a niche backed with chocolate-brown bead board.

553

Corner alcoves provide an ideal setting for holding a collection of Chinese export or other porcelains.

554

Create a tableau of the disparate objects you've collected during your travels.

555

"Show off a collection of vibrant Napoli soft-paste lettuceware in a white breakfront."

—Lee Bierly and Christopher Drake

Create a graphic backdrop for tabletop accessories by making a dense, symmetrical arrangement of small framed artwork.

557

Keep pieces that remind you of children and family members on your bedside table.

558

"Display a collection of Staffordshire pitchers on a tiered serving stand."

—Anthony Baratta and William Diamond

559

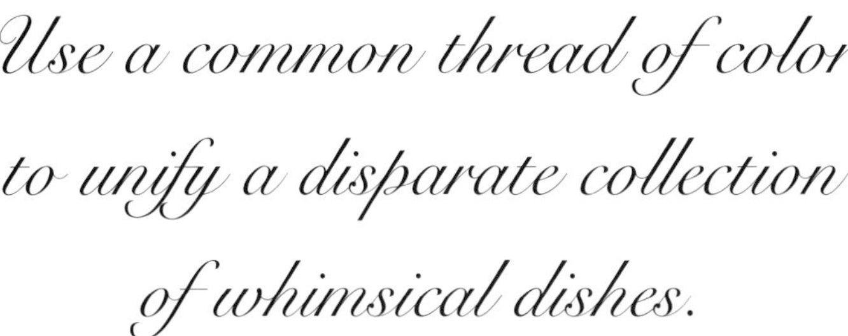

Use a common thread of color to unify a disparate collection of whimsical dishes.

560

An artful arrangement of eclectic treasures makes a thought-provoking setting for a small eating area.

561

"Arrange flea-market finds on a table next to a staircase in a summer house."

—Russell Glover

562

"Show off a mix of Limoges heirlooms, French terra-cotta, and Pottery Barn basics on the shelves of a big attractive hutch in the kitchen."

—Myra Hoefer

563

Build a decorative shelf above a window in a kitchen or breakfast nook and perch a collection of antique porcelain hens on it.

Section Three

Details, Details

564

Enrich your house with layers of personal history.

565

Forgo art in a summer house and use a glue gun to adorn a yard-sale mirror with seashells instead.

566

If you love books but don't have room for them all on proper bookshelves, let them serve as impromptu doorstops, plant stands, and coffee tables.

567

"Be playful: set off a sculptural mid-century modern floor lamp with a kitch vase filled with allium."

—Joe Nahem

568

Choose throw pillows that pick up the tones of your curtain fabric.

569

Keep antique furnishings, classic colors, and patterns fresh by mixing in modern elements, such as black-and-white photography, a flokati rug, and a rich mélange of pillows.

570

"Instead of a mantel, crown a fireplace with one good object, such as an antique carved wood mirror."

—James Lumsden

571

Adorn a beautiful mantel simply.

572

"In lieu of art or bookshelves, flank a fireplace with mirrored bronze window screens."

—Sue Burgess

573

Let a pair of elongated Mexican sconces serve as visual exclamation points.

574

"Never place mirrors opposite one another."

—Jean-Louis Deniot

575

"Give a room with classical elements special charm by introducing details that come as a surprise."
—*Patrice Gruffaz*

576

"Add a fun touch to a home office with vintage glass vases from the 1960s."
—*Benjamin Noriega-Ortiz*

577

"Rejuvenate a room by placing an overscale and geometrically bold mirror over a mantel."

—Tom Scheerer

578

Choose accessories with sculptural shapes that harmonize with the character of your room.

579

Impart the feeling of age to a fireplace by installing a deliciously distressed surround unearthed in a salvage shop.

580

"Top Ikea bookshelves with brass finials for a custom touch."

—Robin Bell Shafer

581

"Always incorporate an element of surprise."

—Victoria Hagan

582

"Look for objects that have great style but have not become decorating clichés."

—Russell Bush

583

"Art is more important than wallcovering."

—Emily Summers

584

"Strip a home of superfluous detail to showcase a collection of fine art and furniture."

—Darryl Carter

French Garden Style
PARIS
GIARDINI E PARCHI ITALIANI
GARDEN BOOK
AMERICAN GARDENS

Chapter Ten

Smart Storage

585

Include a pair of antique or reproduction bookshelves in a style that complements the period of your house.

Eliminating clutter might be impossible, but containing it doesn't have to be. The first step, according to the pros, is to judiciously edit your possessions. Then explore and employ a mix of the many storage solutions available for every room. Free up cabinet space in a small kitchen by hanging pots on a stylish rack overhead. Hide television and stereo equipment in floor-to-ceiling built-in cabinets in a family room. Stow reading glasses and books on a tiered table in a bedroom. Store folded towels on multi-level shelves in your bathroom.

You can build in closets or cabinets, install shelves or cubbies, integrate drawers beneath window seats, slide baskets under beds, stow leather boxes on an overhead ledge, put up a peg rail in a mudroom. The options are endless and the payoff is the peace of mind that order brings.

586

Preserve the clean lines of spare architecture by building in sleek floor-to-ceiling storage cabinets and shelves.

Section One

Containing Clutter

587

Flank a fireplace with built-in cabinets topped with open shelves.

SUPERCHIC
MOVIOLA
SOMEONE ELSE'S MONEY
P.D. James ORIGINAL SIN
PHIL STERN A LIFE'S WORK

588

"When planning for built-ins, determine actual linear feet required for books, magazines, china, linens, clothes, and shoes—then add 10 percent for future growth."

—Celeste Cooper

589

Stow hats in a stack of beautifully trimmed fabric-covered hatboxes.

590

Instead of many towel bars, store folded towels and linens on multi-level shelves.

591

To gain space in a small bath, carve out four- to seven-inch-deep niches for medicine cabinets, open shelves, and toilet-paper holders so they sit flush against the walls rather than project from them.

592

"Be ruthless about editing—especially in a little house."

—Gabriel de la Portilla

593

"I double-stack my books on every shelf, in piles on the stair steps, and use a stack as a makeshift table for a lamp and my decanter of Scotch."

—Keith Irvine

594

"Utilize every inch of wall space in a multipurpose room by installing sturdy floor-to-ceiling bookshelves."

—Walter Radtke and Sabrina Schilcher

595

You can unhook hanging pots and pans more easily than you can dig them out of a dark cupboard.

596

If you have a low ceiling, hang kitchen utensils on hooks on the walls.

597

Hide a dishwasher within a kitchen island.

598

Conceal kitchen cupboards behind a false wall.

599

Store accessories behind a skirted bathroom or kitchen sink.

600

"Give old, cherished, or rare books special status by displaying them in custom-designed bookcases topped with Gothic crown molding and lined with burgundy-colored silk."

—Victoria Klein

601

Stow centerpiece vases and containers in the dining room for easy access.

602

Doll up a bedroom and create a place to hide excess stuff by adding leather or fabric-covered boxes.

603

Let floor-to-ceiling bookshelves define window seat niches in a library.

604

Create storage space beneath a window seat.

PHILIPS
Collins & Aikman
Collins & Aikman
DU PONT
PHOENIX DAY
HUNDRED COUNT
MCS CABLES AND RODS
Decorative Arts
PORTFOLIO OF PRODUCTS
PALMER HARGREAVE
CASTEC
ELKAY
KOHLER
KOHLER

605

"Flank a mantelpiece in a family room with stacked bookcases and fill them with logs, baskets, and books."

—Doug Wilson

606

If you store lots of firewood at a time, consider building floor-to-ceiling shelves on either side of the fireplace.

607

To accommodate growing piles of books, stack them neatly by size with spines lined up under cocktail tables and consoles.

608

Hang attractive seldom-used platters on walls.

609

Install a rolling ladder in front of floor-to-ceiling bookshelves in a library.

610

Store luggage and out-of-season clothes in baskets beneath a bed and hide them with a bedskirt.

611

Let a dining room double as a home office by adding a multifunctional etagere as dual-purpose storage.

612

Stash extra buttons, safety pins, keys, etc., in wooden, silver, or leather bowls or boxes stowed on an above-eye-level shelf.

613

Build in floor-to-ceiling cabinets next to a fireplace to conceal television and stereo equipment.

614

Pile firewood in low oblong baskets or tole tubs.

615

"In a home office, put pens and pencils in a Kartell cart and pile stationary on black-lacquer trays."

—Celeste Cooper

616

"I keep pens and pencils in red, lacquered, tin containers and antique tankards."

— Keith Irvine

617

Too many lampshades make a room look scattered.

618

Never display photos on cocktail tables, which should be free of knick-knacks.

619

For a tidy effect, space framed photos across the mantel and add some candlesticks or vases to the mix.

620

Store jewelry in an antique box or an old piece of furniture with secret drawers.

621

Bedside tables with tiers or drawers let you easily store reading glasses, clocks, books, and magazines.

622

"Convert an American Empire armoire into a bar and stow glasses nearby on a Regency wall shelf."
—Robin Bell Shafer

623

"My bar consists of glasses, bottles, and barware on my grand-mother's silver tray."
—Celeste Cooper

624

If you have vast collections of things, display portions of them until you tire of them—then bump a few bibelots away to make way for others.

625

Install custom cabinets to conceal heating registers and create extra storage.

626

Install a faux board-and-batten wall that swings or slides to conceal storage.

627

In a large space, proudly show off your stuff in cornucopian ways.

Section Two

Closets and Cubbies

628

Craft cubbies in the entryway to a beach house to hold beach paraphernalia.

629

"Add interest to master bedroom closets by fronting them with fabric instead of doors."

—Benjamin Noriega

630

Matching door knobs, hooks, and hardware clean up the look of a closet.

633

Choose bright red or vivid aqua leather boxes to store out-of-season clothing and add a splash of color to a closet.

634

Use an easy-to-clean eggshell finish paint on the inside of the closet.

631

Mirrors on dressing room doors are functional and make the space feel larger.

632

Adjustable shelving systems make it easy to customize closet storage.

635

Install jamb switches, which automatically turn on overhead lights when doors are opened.

636

Add a mirror to the back wall of a closet to reflect more light.

637

"Open up a closet and convert it into an office lined with shelves that contain clutter."

—Anne Marie Vingo

638

"Make use of closet doors by fitting them with full-length mirrors, shoe racks, or hooks for jewelry."

—Linda London

639

"Edit and eliminate four times a year."

—Celeste Cooper

640

"Create separate closets or different zones for like pieces of clothing: one for items you wear every-day, another for dresses, coats and other lengthy garments, one that's shelf-lined for folded sweaters accessories, and another for accessories."

—Linda London

641

Purge yourself of things you no longer wear.

642

"Store athletic gear in a large closet with peg-boards, hanging racks, and bins."

—Celeste Copper

Chapter Eleven

Outdoor Rooms

643

"Add color around a pool by ringing it with sedums, Russian sage, viburnum, hydrangeas, and ornamental grasses."

—Mary Riley Smith

Enrich your routine and expand your horizons by establishing a link with the outdoors. Create a gracious transition between indoors and out with a covered loggia, a screened-in porch, or an awning. Then shape the landscape in accord with your locale and lifestyle.

Turn a terrace into an inviting alfresco dining spot with bistro chairs and a small table. Add fun and function to a pool-side setting with a colorful cabana. Create a quiet place to meditate by building a gazebo on the far reaches of your property. Invite birds and butterflies with birdbaths and buddleia. Please an avid cook with containers full of herbs. Delight yourself with an arbor covered with fragrant climbing roses.

644

"Plant a bed of peonies to add a burst of color against a fieldstone dry wall."

—Richard Bergmann

Section One

Defining Elements of Comfort

645

Create inviting transition zones in a garden with plant-draped pergolas, stone paved terraces, and grassy walking paths.

646

Blur the distinction between indoors and outdoors with a lanai (a roofed patio), a Hawaiian technique.

647

"Establish a series of outdoor living spots—a loggia for lounging on hot days, a dining table under apple trees, and a small parterre where two can talk."

—Mia Lehrer

648

"Tie colorful hammocks to trees to entice guests to explore your grounds."

—Sherry Donghia

649

"Create an outdoor living room on a deck with an all-weather fabric-covered sofa."

—Diana Vinoly

650

"Let a guest house porch double as an open-air space for summer dinner parties as well as a pool-side lounge area."

—Tim Clarke

651

Install a bench in a fragrant herb garden so you can savor the scents of oregano, mint, thyme, artemesia, and salvia.

652

Highlight a courtyard between a main house and guest house with an arched gate strewn with climbing roses.

653

"Convert a lobster crate into a table and surround it with metal chairs in a rustic screened porch."

—Gary Henkin

654

"I like to create many conversational areas rather than corralling people into one big clump."

—Sherry Donghia

655

A mix of table linen and chair cushion patterns keeps an outdoor table from looking too studied.

656

Top a daybed on a veranda with mosquito netting.

657

Enclose a private sanctuary with a decorative fence festooned with a mask and climbing plants such as nasturtiums and golden hop.

658

Add character to a porch by adding a white-painted vintage table topped with Formica.

659

Create a relaxed feeling on a terrace or patio by incorporating eclectic pieces gathered in your travels.

660

Create a comfortable seating area beneath a loggia with slipcovered chairs and a table on which to set a drink or a book.

661

Mow a path to a tiny pond-front beach and set a few chairs along the water's edge.

662

A loggia with French doors offers a gracious transition between indoors and outdoors and can tie separate wings of the house together.

Section Two

Introducing and Controlling Light

663

Set an outdoor bench beneath an arbor covered with climbing roses to shield it from the sun.

664

"Create intimacy and shield family and friends from sunlight by surrounding a porch with flowing, full-length curtains."

—*Celia Cabral Domenech*

665

"When it starts getting dark at an outdoor party, put a big hurricane lamp on the table and a votive by each place setting."

—*Sherry Donghia*

666

Install decorative lanterns to add character and illumination on a terrace.

667

Create a shaded dining spot beneath an upstairs porch.

668

Shelter a pool pavilion from the sun with white, floor-to-ceiling curtains in washable polyester.

669

Surround the terrace of a city dwelling with decorative lattice to create shade and privacy.

670

"Direct a stroll through a garden in accord with the time of day to avoid marring a view with sunlight shining in one's eyes."

—David Hicks

671

In a house in the tropics, install an abundance of awnings, shutters, curtains, and French doors that can be adjusted to deal with the sunlight.

672

Shield a terrace from direct sunlight with a teakwood arcade covered with clematis, roses, and wisteria.

Section Three

Plants and Garden Ornaments

673

If you like to cook, cultivate a thriving herb garden.

674

"Soften the formality of raised flower beds with a curved mown path that invites exploration."

—Gina Price

675

"Break up a garden with low straight hedges of yew and boxwood to create the illusion of distinct spaces that make the garden look larger."

—*Lisa Bynon*

676

"Imbue a garden with a sense of age by planting it with olive trees."

—*Mia Lehrer*

677

"For seasonal color in a small garden, plant a shadbush (*Amelanchier arborea*, zones 4-9) next to an Eastern redbud (*Cercis canadensis*, zones 4-9)—the shadbush produces clouds of small white flowers that are followed by blue edible fruit and apricot-hued fall foliage, while the redbud's lavender flowers of early spring are replaced by heart-shaped leaves that turn a pretty yellow after frost."

—*Katherine Whiteside*

678

Enhance a winter view with outdoor sculpture.

679

"Use fountains to cool the air and mask outdoor noises."

—Douglas Dodd

680

"Plant flowering trees to bring texture, structure, and color to the garden in every season."

—Katherine Whiteside

681

Enhance a grand geometric design with rows of clipped crab-apple trees surrounded by gravel paths.

682

"Add interest to a fountain by surrounding it with a mosaic path of pebbles."

—Harry Nelson

683

Trimmed hedges and parterres offer a study in shades of green.

684

The lateral boughs of crab-apple trees (*Malus floribunda*, zones 5-8) yield masses of pink buds that open to snowy white flowers in spring, then produce deep yellow fruit and leaves in autumn.

685

Sustain a zingy palette through the seasons with tulips and narcissi, peonies, Canterbury bells and rock roses, spiky hostas, sculptural euphorbia, and sorbus berries.

686

Add a sculptural touch to an outdoor seating area with a collection of succulents or other shapely plants in interesting pots.

687

"Plants in containers can transform problem spaces, such as barren areas where there isn't any soil or shady areas too dark for conventional beds."

—Ken Druse

688

Turn a water-logged yard into a boggy sanctuary that welcomes mallards, herons, and other wildlife.

689

"Clip a bevy of yews to create a 'cone folly,' which becomes especially graphic after a snowfall."

—Richard Bergmann

690

"Create a garden axis by planting a birch tree as a distant focal point that forms a triangle with two white hydrangeas."

—Katherine Whiteside

691

"Create symmetrical vistas of contrasting greens with perspectives that lead the eye from the house to the horizon."

—*David Hicks*

692

"A garden must respond to the architecture of the house as well as the site."

—*Wade Graham*

693

"In October, plant some crocus chrysanthus, which will bloom and provide color in late winter."

—*Katherine Whiteside*

694

"To eliminate mosquitos in containers holding water plants, add goldfish, which eat up every yucky bug in the water."

—*Katherine Whiteside*

695

Install a Chinese pavilion amid apple and oak trees.

696

"A garden has to be useful, not just decorative—it has to offer something to eat, something to cut, and it has to smell and look good."

—Patricia Kluge

697

"Cultivate an herb garden, even if all you have room for is some small pots—a few fresh sprigs add so much flavor to food."

—Sherry Donghia

"Enclose a back garden with a wall that matches your house, edge it with a low hedge of boxwood, and cover it with creeping fig."

—Timothy Adcock

699

"Introduce a formal boxwood-trimmed brick path to link the different parts of a multifaceted garden."

—Mary Riley Smith

700

"Integrate a pair of existing palm trees with a poolscape by framing them in a travertine planter accented with river stones and barrel cacti."

—Steve Martino

701

Create a soothing ambience with the slow trickle of water in a sunlit fountain.

702

"Create a good-looking vegetable garden by starting with four beds, covering paths in between with straw, pine needles, or wood chips, and growing annuals like Johnny-jump-up (*Viola Tricolor*) and brightly colored sweet peas among vegetables like leeks and asparagus."

—Katherine Whiteside

703

"Plant an old birdbath with petunias."

—Patricia Thorpe

Menu
Cream of Chestnut Soup
with Pecan Stuffing
Purée of Potato and Celery Root
Glazed Carrots
Brussel Sprouts with Pancetta and Cream

Chapter Twelve

All-Occasion Entertaining

Dress up a holiday table with a centerpiece redolent of forest pine trees and snow.

People may make the party, but they'll have more fun if the ambience is appropriately festive. Whether you're hosting a formal dinner, an informal cocktail event, or a casual birthday party for a cadre of kids—start by creating an atmosphere that reinforces the occasion. Choose white or ecru linen, cotton, or damask for a formal holiday meal and add small bouquets of red roses and porcelain baskets of red grapes, apples, and plums. Cover an informal Thanksgiving table with a paisley shawl and top it with mounds of gourds in bowls. Place a patchwork tablecloth made from fabric remnants on an outdoor table—and have hurricane lamps on hand and ready to light as soon as night begins to fall.

705

Set up a large zinc-topped picnic table and folding French park chairs on a deck for an alfresco meal.

Section One

Creating Ambience

706

"For a sense of easy elegance in a dining room, choose Swedish-inspired furnishings or reproductions."

—Annika Bogart Elias

707

Sunny yellow walls and upholstery infuse an old-fashioned dining room with contemporary energy.

708

"Make a statement with a large work of art."

—Darryl Carter

709

Create an air of classic comfort by pairing a country French table with painted American Windsor chairs and an antique American wood-and-wire chandelier.

710

"Make an ordinary dining table look more interesting by surrounding it with mismatched chairs."

—Robin Bell Shafer

711

"Place candles everywhere, including bathrooms—guests look better and feel happier in candlelight."

—Sherry Donghia

712

Create a sense of enclosure for an alfresco meal by setting up a table and chairs near walls festooned with ivy and jasmine.

713

Finish dining room walls with a color taken from your china.

714

Set up a table and bistro chairs in the shade of a large tree.

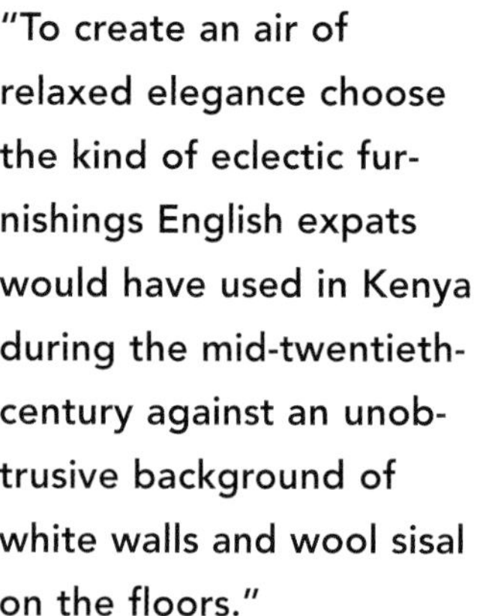

715

"To create an air of relaxed elegance choose the kind of eclectic furnishings English expats would have used in Kenya during the mid-twentieth-century against an unobtrusive background of white walls and wool sisal on the floors."

—Mary McDonald

716

"To make a dining room seem more intimate, employ an artist to paint faux wainscoting, beams, and ceiling coffers."

—David Netto

718

"Cover the walls of a formal dining room in a bold color to set off eighteenth-century Hepplewhite chairs."

—Pierre Serrurier and Imogen Taylor

719

Visually enlarge a small dining room by installing mirror-paned fixed doors on one wall.

717

"Present an alfresco buffet as a graphic, eye-filling feast."

—Paola Navone

720

Dress up a swimming pool wall with a curtain of prostrate rosemary.

721

Evoke a holiday ambience by placing potted paperwhites in front of a fireplace and a rustic wreath over the mantel.

722

"For a Halloween party for children, use floral spray and spray paint in abundance to decorate temporary walls or props like jack-o'-lanterns."

—*Carolyne Roehm*

723

Instead of an ordinary tree stand, set a Christmas tree into something that holds its own, such as a handsome iron urn.

Section Two

Table Settings and Linens

724

Give a formal dining table a casual touch by topping it with a few woven baskets filled with ivy.

725

"Dispense with formality and entertain with uncomplicated flair."

—*Tamasin Day Lewis*

726

Consider topping a table with a beautiful lace shawl.

727

"Add zest to a Southern holiday table with topiaries of kumquat and lemon leaves nestled into a pair of Choisy blue-and-white cachepots."

—*Carolyne Roehm*

728

For fall parties, stick to muted earth tones such as brown, rust, pumpkin, cognac, burnt umber, orange, and sienna.

729

For a formal meal, choose white, off-white, or ecru linen or cotton damask or matelasse.

730

"For an informal Thanksgiving dinner, top a worn wood table with earthenware, heavy stemware, and hunt-inspired dinner plates."

—Carolyn Roehm

731

"Use a paisley shawl as an inspired alternative to a standard linen tablecloth."

—Carolyne Roehm

732

"Use heavy carved wood tassels to hold down the top cloth on an outdoor table."

—John Dransfield and Geoffrey Ross

733

"Make a patchwork tablecloth from fabric remnants for an outdoor table."

—*Sherry Donghia*

734

"Wrap wine and water buckets in colorful fabrics."

—*Sherry Donghia*

736

Your best porcelain, stemware, and silver are expected at a formal dinner.

737

Branch away from red and green—set a holiday table with vintage lusterware in shades of cream and robin's egg blue.

738

Lay a white linen-wrapped table with antique glass and simple white china for Christmas dinner party.

735

"Create place cards with a nautical theme for a sunset cruise buffet dinner."

—Vincent Scotto

Section Three

Centerpieces and Accents

739

"Single-flower arrangements in silver vases make a stunning contemporary statement."

—Carolyne Roehm

740

"Chartreuse is a bold accent in an autumnal bouquet."

—*Carolyne Roehm*

741

"For a formal Thanksgiving dinner, choose roses in rich reds, fiery oranges, and terra-cotta."

—*Carolyne Roehm*

742

Dress up a Thanksgiving table with mounds of gourds in bowls and on silver trays along with small bunches of roses.

743

Try mixing chrysanthemums, with their stylized shapes, with skimmia, seeded eucalyptus, hypericum berries, and snow berries on a harvest table—shiny green magnolia, lemon, and camellia leaves add lush contrast.

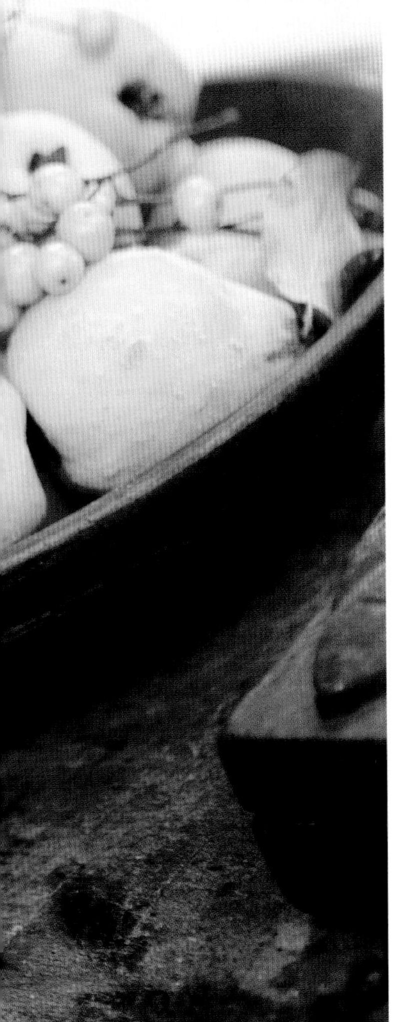

744

"For an autumnal setting, take a cue from seventeenth-century Dutch still lifes and toss in some fruit."

—Carolyne Roehm

745

"Add panache to a console or sideboard by massing billy balls in a pewter chalice found at a flea market."

—David Stark

746

Create an alfresco still life by composing pretty silver, china, and majolica with a contemporary vase filled with peonies.

747

Adorn a snapper-shaped Christmas favor with single fresh rose.

748

"Chrysanthemums, asters, viburnum, chokeberry, hypericum, bittersweet, rosehips, crab-apples, milkweed, shafts of wheat, poppy pods, and colorful autumn leaves make wonderful casual fall bouquets."

—Carolyne Roehm

749

For fun, juxtapose yellow poppies, daffodils, ranunculus, and mimosa in a coffee can.

—David Stark

750

Grapes, apples, pomegranates, small pears, and persimmons add interest to any bouquet.

Photography Credits

Page 3 Jon Ellis
Page 3 Joshua Sheldon
Page 6 Jeff McNamara
Page 6 Rene Stoeltie
Page 7 Pieter Estersohn
Page 12 Laura Resen
Pages 14–15 Gordon Beall
Pages 16–17 Dana Gallagher
Page 18 John M. Hall
Page 19 Gordon Beall
Page 20 Oberto Gili
Page 21 Tim Street-Porter
Pages 22–23 Gordon Beall
Page 22 Tria Giovan
Page 23 Gordon Beall
Page 26 Laura Resen
Page 27 Jacques Dirand
Pages 28–29 Tim Street-Porter
Page 30 Pieter Estersohn
Page 31 Tim Street-Porter
Pages 32–33 Victoria Person
Page 34 James Mortimer
Page 35 Eric Bowman
Pages 36–37 Gordon Beall
Page 38 Peter Estersohn
Page 39 Simon Upton
Page 40 Eric Piasecki
Page 41 Dana Gallagher
Pages 42–43 Gordon Beall
Page 44 Simon Upton
Page 45 Tria Giovan
Page 46 Simon Upton
Pages 48–49 Peter Murdoch
Page 50–51 Marco Ricca
Page 53 Oberto Gili
Page 54 Lisa Romerein
Page 55 Peter Murdoch
Page 56 Roger Davies
Page 57 Pieter Estersohn
Page 58 Gordon Beall
Page 59 Tim Street-Porter
Page 60 Dana Gallagher
Page 61 Laura Resen
Page 62 Oberto Gili
Page 63 Hugh Stewart
Page 64 Gordon Beall
Page 65 Tim Street-Porter
Page 66 Gabi Zimmerman
Page 67 Nedjeljko Matura
Page 68 Carlos Emilio
Page 69 Simon Upton
Pages 70–71 Oberto Gili
Page 72 Lisa Romerein
Page 73 Roger Davies
Page 75 Gordon Beall
Page 77 Tim Beddow
Page 78 Joshua Sheldon
Page 78 Joshua Sheldon
Page 79 Lisa Romerein
Pages 80–81 Tim Street –Porter
Page 82 Tim Street-Porter
Page 83 Tim Street-Porter
Page 84 Oberto Gili
Pages 86–87 Victoria Pearson
Page 88 Gordon Beall
Page 89 Simon Upton
Page 90 Rene Stoeltie
Page 91 Tria Giovan
Pages 92–93 Tim Beddow
Page 94 Gordon Beall
Page 95 Gordon Beall
Pages 96–97 Grey Crawford
Pages 98–99 Jeff McNamara
Pages 100–101 Michel Arnaud
Page 102 Eric Roth
Page 103 Roger Davies
Page 104 Michel Arnaud
Page 105 Tim Street-Porter
Page 106 Tria Giovan
Page 107 Eric Bowman
Pages 108–109 Eric Bowman
Page 110 Sam Gray
Page 111 Vicente Wolf
Page 112 Carlos Emilio
Page 113 Jeff McNamara
Page 114 Eric Boman
Page 115 Tim Street-Porter
Page 116 Alex Hemer
Page 117 Tria Giovan
Page 118 Simon Upton
Page 119 Pieter Estersohn
Page 120 J. Savage Gibson
Page 121 Gordon Beall
Pages 122–123 Carlos Domenech
Page 124 Coleen Duffley
Page 125 Victoria Pearson
Page 126 Joshua McHugh
Page 127 Elizabeth Glaskow
Pages 128–129 Carlos Domenech
Page 130 Von der Schulenberg
Page 131 Roger Davies
Page 132 Roger Davies
Page 133 Oberto Gili
Page 135 Pieter Estersohn
Page 134 Nigel Young
Page 135 Gordon Beall
Page 136 Carlos Emilio
Page 137 Tria Giovan
Pages 138–139 Dominique Vorillon
Page 140 Gordon Beall
Page 141 Tria Giovan
Page 142 Simon Upton
Page 143 Simon Upton
Page 144 Eric Bowman
Page 145 Tria Giovan
Page 146 Dana Gallagher
Page 147 Lisa Romerein
Page 148 Tim Street-Porter
Pages 149 Jeff McNamara
Pages 150–151 Eric Bowman
Page 152–153 Antoine Bootz
Page 154–155 Simon Upton
Page 156 Tria Giovan
Page 157 Simon Upton
Page 158 Oberto Gili
Page 159 Grey Crawford

Pages 160–161 Peter Margonelli
Page 162 Gordon Beall
Page 164 Peter Murdoch
Page 166 Tim Street-Porter
Page 167 Sam Gray
Page 168 Robert Hiemstra
Page 169 Gabi Zimmerman
Page 170 Sang An
Page 170 Sang An
Page 171 Tim Street-Porter
Pages 172–173 Joshua McHugh
Page 174 Victoria Pearson
Page 175 Victoria Pearson
Page 176 Pieter Estersohn
Page 177 Peter Margonelli
Page 178 Tim Street-Porter
Page 179 Maura McEvoy
Page 180 Simon Upton
Page 181 Bruce Buck
Page 182 Simon Upton
Pages 184–185 Eric Piasecki
Pages 186–187 Laura Resen
Page 188 Victoria Pearson
Page 189 Dana Gallagher
Page 190 Jon Jensen
Page 191 David Phelps
Page 192 Victoria Pearson
Page 193 Gordon Beall
Page 194 Gordon Beall
Page 195 Simon Upton
Page 195 Oberto Gili
Pages 196–197 Gordon Beall
Page 198 Carlos Domenech
Page 199 Carlos Domenech
Page 200 Jeff McNamara
Page 201 Victoria Pearson
Page 202 Carlos Domenech
Page 204 Victoria Pearson
Page 204 Tria Giovan
Page 205 Carlos Domenech
Page 206 Oberto Gili
Page 207 Dana Gallagher
Page 208 Victoria Pearson
Page 209 Charles Maraia
Page 210 Oberto Gili
Page 211 Dominique Vorillon
Page 212 Tria Giovan
Page 213 Nigel Young
Pages 214–215 Tria Giovan
Pages 216 Victoria Pearson
Pages 218–219 Laura Resen
Page 220 John M. Hall
Page 221 Tria Giovan
Page 222 Tria Giovan
Page 223 Gordon Beall
Pages 224–225 Dominique Vorillon
Page 226 Victoria Pearson
Page 227 Victoria Pearson
Page 228 Tim Street-Porter
Page 229 Gordon Beall
Pages 230–231 Tom Crane
Page 232 Victoria Pearson
Page 233 Dana Gallagher
Pages 234–235 Eric Bowman
Page 236 Gordon Beall
Page 237 Jacques Dirand
Page 238 Dana Gallagher
Page 239 John Ellis
Page 240 Gordon Beall
Page 242 Victoria Pearson
Page 243 Eric Piasecki
Page 244 Melissa Punch
Page 245 Victoria Pearson
Page 246 Victoria Pearson
Page 247 Peter Margonelli
Page 248 Tim Street-Porter
Page 249 Victoria Pearson
Page 250 Victoria Pearson
Page 251 Laura Resen
Page 252 Brendan Paul
Pages 254–255 Tria Giovan
Pages 256–257 Michel Arnaud
Pages 258 Roger Davies
Page 259 Tim Street-Porter
Page 260 Eric Bowman
Page 260 Simon Upton
Page 261 Tria Giovan
Page 262 Tim Street-Porter
Page 263 Sam Gray
Page 264 Dana Gallagher
Page 265 Tim Beddow
Page 266 Gordon Beall
Page 267 Simon Upton
Page 268 Gordon Beall
Page 270 Lizzie Himmel
Page 270 Lizzie Himmel
Page 271 Brendan Paul
Page 272 Dana Gallagher
Page 272 Thibault Jeanson
Page 273 Charles Maraia
Page 273 Oberto Gili
Page 274 Laura Resen
Page 274 Victoria Pearson
Page 275 Tim Beddow
Page 276 Polly Eltes
Page 277 Tim Street-Porter
Page 278 Jacques Dirand
Page 280 Tria Giovan
Page 280 Dana Gallagher
Page 281 Victoria Pearson
Page 282 Tim Street-Porter
Page 283 Carlos Domenech
Page 283 Thibault Jeanson
Page 284 Gabi Zimmerman
Page 286 Luke White
Page 287 Gordon Beall
Page 288 Victoria Pearson
Page 289 Oberto Gili
Page 289 Charles Maraia
Page 290 Simon Upton
Page 290 Thibault Jeanson
Page 292 Tara Striano
Pages 294–295 Eric Piasecki
Page 296 Oberto Gili
Page 298 Joshua Sheldon
Page 298 Luca Trovato
Page 299 Tim Street-Porter
Page 300 Roger Davies
Page 301 Dana Gallagher
Pages 302–303 Gabi Zimmerman
Page 304 Sam Gray
Page 305 Dana Gallagher
Page 306 David Duncan Livingston
Page 307 Tara Striano
Pages 308–309 Tria Giovan
Page 310 Tim Street-Porter
Page 311 Eric Piasecki
Page 312 Joshua McHugh

Page 313 Tim Street-Porter
Pages 314–315 Tim Street-Porter
Pages 316–317 Eric Roth
Pages 318–319 Simon Upton
Pages 320–321 Eric Piasecki
Page 322 Coleen Duffley
Page 323 Gordon Beall
Page 324 Simon Upton
Page 325 Tria Giovan
Page 326 Roger Davies
Page 327 Laura Resen
Page 328 Tim Beddow
Page 329 Tria Giovan
Page 329 Richard Bryant/Arcaid
Page 330 Laura Resen
Page 330 Antoine Bootz
Page 331 Simon Upton
Pages 332–333 Dana Gallagher
Page 334 Tim Street-Porter
Page 334 Laura Resen
Page 333 Coleen Duffley
Page 336 Victoria Pearson
Page 337 Michel Arnaud
Page 338 Vicente Wolf
Page 339 Dana Gallagher
Page 339 Thibault Jeanson
Page 340 Tria Giovan
Page 341 Roger Davies
Page 341 Jeremy Samuelson
Page 342 Laura Resen
Page 342 Jeremy Samuelson
Page 343 Tria Giovan
Page 344 Oberto Gili
Page 346 Roger Davies
Page 346 Lisa Romerein
Page 347 John Ellis
Page 348 Pieter Estersohn
Page 349 Rene Stoeltie
Page 350 Simon Upton
Page 350 Gordon Beall
Pages 352–353 Erik Kvalsvik
Pages 354–355 Peter Aaron/Esto
Page 356 John Hall
Page 358 Jacques Dirand
Page 358 Paul Whicheloe
Page 359 Paul Whicheloe
Page 360 Nedjeljko Matura
Page 361 Tim Street-Porter
Page 362 Roger Davies
Page 363 Pieter Estersohn
Page 363 Jon Jensen
Page 364 Eric Piasecki
Page 365 Gordon Beall
Page 365 Eric Roth
Page 366 Tim Street-Porter
Page 366 Laura Resen
Page 367 J. Savage Gibson
Page 369 Tria Giovan
Page 372 Peter Murdoch
Page 372 Jacques Dirand
Page 373 Jon Jensen
Page 373 Victoria Pearson
Page 374 Richard Felber
Pages 376–377 Karen Bussolini
Pages 378–379 John Hall
Page 380 Tim Street-Porter
Page 381 Oberto Gili
Page 382 Victoria Pearson
Page 383 Marina Schinz
Page 384 Peter Murdock
Page 385 Laura Resen
Page 386 Clive Nichols
Page 387 John Hall
Page 387 Michel Arnaud
Pages 388–389 Marion Brenner
Page 390 Carlos Domenech
Page 391 Lisa Romerein
Page 392 Eric Bowman
Page 392 Michael James O'Brien
Page 393 Carlos Emilio
Page 394 Dana Hyde
Page 395 Christopher Baker
Pages 396–397 Tim Street-Porter
Page 398 Pieter Estersohn
Page 399 Pieter Estersohn
Page 399 Tria Giovan
Page 400 Gordon Beall
Page 401 Karen Bussolini
Page 402 Michael James O'Brien
Page 402 Michael James O'Brien
Page 403 Ericka McConnell
Page 404 Ken Druse
Page 405 Judith Bromley
Page 405 Karen Bussolini
Page 406 Dana Hyde
Page 407 Vincent Motte
Page 408 Christopher Baker
Page 408 John M. Hall
Page 409 Richard Felber
Page 410 Jose Picayo
Page 412–413 Oberto Gili
Pages 414–415 Victoria Pearson
Page 416 Dana Gallagher
Page 418 Oberto Gili
Page 419 Jon Ellis
Page 419 Tria Giovan
Page 420 Victoria Pearson
Page 421 Dana Gallagher
Page 422 Jacques Dirand
Page 422 Jeff McNamara
Page 423 Tim Street-Porter
Page 424 Molly Chapellet
Page 426 Stefan Studer
Page 426 Polly Eltes
Page 427 Ann Stratton
Pages 428–429 Tim Street-Porter
Page 430 William Mappem
Page 430 Jose Picayo
Page 431 Sylvie Becquet
Page 431 Sylvie Becquet
Page 432 Dana Gallagher
Page 434 William Meppem
Pages 436–437 Sylvie Becquet
Page 438 Sylvie Becquet
Page 439 Sylvie Becquet
Page 439 Ann Stratton
Page 441 Natasha Milne
Page 441 Ann Stratton

Index